I0605712

The Essential...
Harry Styles

Published in 2026
by Gemini Gift Books
Part of Gemini Books Group

Based in Woodbridge and London
Marine House, Tide Mill Way,
Woodbridge, Suffolk IP12 1AP
United Kingdom
www.geminibooks.com

ISBN 978-1-78675-198-0

A CIP catalogue record for this book is available from the British Library.

Manufacturer's EU Representative: Eurolink Compliance Limited, 25 Herbert Place, Dublin, D02 AY86, Republic of Ireland. admin@eurolink-europe.ie

Printed in China
10 9 8 7 6 5 4 3 2 1

This book was first published as *Harry Styles* in 2024. This abridged edition is published in 2026.

The Essential...
Harry Styles

UNOFFICIAL AND UNAUTHORIZED

ANNIE ZALESKI

Contents

Bigsby

Introduction

On the surface, Harry Styles' path to stardom looks a lot like that of another teen idol: *NSYNC's Justin Timberlake. Both men catapulted to global fame with their former bands – and became fan favourites in the process – and both launched solo careers on their own terms. In the early to mid-2000s, Timberlake created cutting-edge pop/R'n'B collaborations with futuristic beatmakers like Timbaland and The Neptunes; Styles, meanwhile, chose to draw from timeless retro sounds, including 1970s folk, soul and rock, as well as 1980s pop.

Dig a little deeper, however, and Styles' artistic ascent has parallels to the musical careers of several other legends. His willingness to take musical risks and stay true to his muse echoes George Michael; the latter also left a successful pop group (the 1980s duo Wham!) for the freedom of being an iconoclastic pop star who cherished artistic integrity. Styles' approach to music also calls to mind the Beatles icon Paul McCartney. Not only is Macca an adventurous solo artist – look no further than synthesizer experiments such as 'Temporary Secretary' – but after the Beatles parted ways, McCartney reinvented himself as the leader of another band, Wings; and Styles himself now performs live with a core group of stellar musicians. In a more contemporary vein, perhaps

PAGE 4 & LEFT Harry Styles performs onstage at Coachella in April 2022.

there's also a little of Madonna and Lady Gaga in the way Styles has branched out beyond music into fashion and movies.

Then again, it's also quite unfair to compare Styles to *anybody*, as he's a singular artist who has carved out a unique path in the world. His solo albums reshape the boundaries of pop music, challenging listeners to think about mainstream modern music in a new way. Styles' approach to fashion eschews strict gender binaries; he's appeared on the cover of *Vogue* wearing a dress and sported colourful, tattoo-baring jumpsuits as stagewear while on tour. He's also never been afraid to try new things, such as be a last-minute fill-in host on a late-night network TV talk show. And Styles empowers fans to embrace their true selves in genuine, earnest ways – among other things, a favourite bit of concert chat is, "Please feel free to be whoever it is that you want to be in this room tonight" – which has made his shows supportive, inclusive, community-gathering places.

He also loved being a part of his original band, One Direction, which released a steady string of albums brimming with joyful pop tunes, like 'What Makes You Beautiful' and 'Best Song Ever' before going on hiatus in 2016. "When you leave a band or boy band, you feel like you have to go the complete other direction and kind of say, 'Don't worry everyone! I hated it! It wasn't me!'," he said in the documentary *Harry Styles: Behind the Album*, which was released in conjunction with his 2017 self-titled debut album. "I loved it. I wouldn't be here if it wasn't for that band. And I don't feel like I have to apologize for that."

Indeed, Styles has navigated the evolution from boy band phenom to solo star rather seamlessly. Part of that is his grounded upbringing, which has kept him level-headed. "He's just the same as he has always been," his mother Anne Twist told *The Daily Mail* in April 2023. "As a very little boy, he was very much like he is now, just a smaller version." Styles' music reflects this self-assurance. "He's very authentic to himself," Twist continued. "He takes his influences from what he feels, what he's listened to, what

RIGHT Harry Styles, December 2015.

he likes. He's not thinking, 'Right, I need to make this song for this particular demographic.' He does what feels right to him – and it seems to be universally appreciated."

This intuitive way of making music has led to solo albums that *feel* modern – and fit right in on Top 40 radio – but don't necessarily conform to dominant contemporary trends. Styles' debut album was heavily influenced by 1970s rock and pop; his follow-up album, 2019's *Fine Line*, was inspired partly by the innovative genre-shapeshifter Joni Mitchell. And 2022's *Harry's House* touched on funk, soft rock and R'n'B, among other genres.

Outside of music, Styles has remained true to himself and his moral compass, advocating for things like gun control, Black Lives Matter and LGBTQ+ rights. His support for the queer community predates his solo career: during a 2014 One Direction tour stop in St Louis, Missouri, Styles wore a Michael Sam jersey, in support of the first openly gay player drafted in the NFL (National Football League).

Unsurprisingly, Styles has had a marked influence on the music world as a whole. Both Milky Chance and Jorja Smith have covered his 2022 hit, 'As It Was', while the 1980s icon Rick Astley – another pop star who knows a little something about success at a young age – also covered the tune at a New Year's Eve performance in 2023. What Harry Styles will do next in his life *and* career is anyone's guess – but you can be sure that whatever it is will be interesting, unexpected *and* colourful.

LEFT Performing onstage with One Direction at Z100's Jingle Ball 2012, Madison Square Garden, New York City.

OVERLEAF Harry Styles: Live On Tour, Madison Square Garden, 21 June 2018, in New York City.

BLACK LIVES MATTER
BLACK LIVES MATTER

65998

CHAPTER 1

STORY OF MY LIFE

PAGE 14 Harry Styles auditions for *The X Factor*, 2010.

LEFT Harry Styles at the age of three.

Harry Styles is standing at a microphone, sporting shaggy hair and a dapper suit, ready for one of the biggest performances of his life. As his band kicks into Bryan Adams' 'Summer of '69', he looks down intently, clearly concentrating on making sure his vocals are on point. The focus pays off: when Styles starts singing, he sounds self-assured, nailing every note of the rocker with hints of vibrato and an abundance of passion.

At first, a couple of women near the front of the stage are distracted – talking to each other, fixing their hair, and looking for their friends. By the second verse, however, Styles and the band have won them over, and they've started gleefully dancing and pogo-ing. Even Styles hitting a few rough notes – understandably, since 'Summer of '69' does have some difficult high-register moments – can't stop the good vibes.

Incredibly enough, this footage wasn't from a One Direction gig or a solo concert – but of 16-year-old Harry Styles singing lead for his scrappy rock band White Eskimo at the wedding of a friend's mother. The performance was a rather last-minute gig. Styles later recalled the group ended up having to learn 25 songs (including Bob Marley tunes requested by the bride) in a matter of days. The quartet was only paid £160 – equivalent to a little less than US $200 – split between the four of them.

At the time, White Eskimo was earning some local notoriety; among other things, they won the 2009 Battle of the Bands at Styles' school, Holmes Chapel Comprehensive School in Cheshire. They were also dabbling in writing original tunes, including one

LEFT Harry Styles holds a photograph of himself as a young boy as he greets fans during a visit to his home town of Holmes Chapel, in Cheshire, England.

about luggage called 'Gone in a Week', which Styles could still quote verbatim years later.

This stint with White Eskimo gave Styles a small taste of music success, enough to make him crave more time in the spotlight. However, his early upbringing didn't necessarily point to him becoming a global superstar. Styles was born on 1 February 1994, in Worcestershire, England, the second child of Anne Twist and Desmond "Des" Styles. (His sister Gemma had arrived four years earlier.) By all accounts, he was an outgoing, polite kid who had a lot of friends and got along well with others.

Growing up in Holmes Chapel, a village the family moved to in Cheshire, England, Styles soaked up all different kinds of music. He loved Elvis Presley's tender 1960 hit, 'The Girl of My Best Friend'; in fact, this was the first song he recorded when his grandfather gave him a karaoke machine as an eighth-birthday present. His mother gravitated toward more modern pop artists, such as the 1980s-inspired Savage Garden, jazz-influenced Norah Jones, and country icon Shania Twain. In contrast, his dad, who worked as a financial advisor, loved classic rock bands such as the Rolling Stones, Queen, Pink Floyd and Fleetwood Mac. The latter group loomed particularly large in his world.

"In my family, we listened at home, we listened in the car, we listened wherever we could," Styles said in his 2019 speech inducting Fleetwood Mac's Stevie Nicks into the Rock & Roll Hall of Fame. '"Dreams" was the first song I knew all the words to, before I really knew what all the words meant. I thought it was a song about the weather. But I knew it was a beautiful song about the weather."

"[My dad would] play Elvis Presley to death, the Stones. I'd sing along to that and he'd say, 'You're going to be famous'."

RIGHT At the BRIT Awards after-party with his mother, Anne, in 2013.

It's clear in hindsight to see how these formative listening experiences inspired Styles and influenced the music he would later create. But early on, both parents recognized their son's potential. "I used to listen to a lot of the music [my dad] was playing," Styles told *Rolling Stone*. "He'd play Elvis Presley to death, the Stones. I'd sing along to that and he'd say, 'You're going to be famous', or whatever." His mum, meanwhile, once corrected Simon Cowell after the *X-Factor* judge claimed that mothers might have a skewed perspective on whether their kids have talent. "He said, 'Mums don't always know'," she told *The Daily Mail*. "But I always thought [Harry] had something."

Indeed, this wasn't a case of parental bias. At age five, Styles made his stage debut at Hermitage Primary School in Holmes Chapel, portraying a church-dwelling mouse named Barney. An adorable video of this performance captures Styles' preternatural charisma. It's not terribly obvious that the tiny child onstage is a future superstar, but his reactions and hand gestures are crisp and on beat – no small feat for such an acting novice.

In the coming years, young Styles would experience some big life changes, starting with his parents divorcing when he was seven years old. Although the break-up's aftermath was as positive as it could be – "Feeling supported and loved by my parents never changed," he said years later – Styles was particularly close to his mum; in fact, post-divorce, he and Gemma went along with her when she moved out of the village. "Since I've been 10, it's kind of felt like – protect mum at all costs," he told *Rolling Stone* in 2017. "My mum is very strong. She has the greatest heart."

Styles was nine years old when his mother remarried, to a man named John Cox. The couple operated a pub in Cheshire called the Antrobus Arms, and Styles lived above the pub. "I remember the first night, it was like a night where a band was playing, and I just thought, 'How am I going to get to sleep?'" Styles told *Rolling Stone*, referencing the noise emanating from the pub. However, he added that he eventually became used to hearing the music – and even learned some guitar basics from a rocker who "used to be in Deep Purple or something" that occasionally played at the pub.

Years later, Cox reminisced that Styles unsurprisingly loved the Antrobus Arms' convivial atmosphere, and would frequently hang out with the adults. "He was the centre of attention," he told *The Mirror*. "He was really lively and would run around the pub, with all the customers fussing over him." Cox also fondly remembers singing Frank Sinatra's '(Theme from) New York, New York' with a young Styles at another pub's karaoke night. "He is a down-to-earth kid, and always has been."

When he was a teenager, Styles would experience yet another big life change. Cox and his mother split up, which led to a move back to Holmes Chapel. Not long after, Styles' mum met and started dating a man named Robin Twist. This time, it was her turn to be protective of her kids; Styles recalled, in the One Direction autobiography *Dare to Dream*, that she was cautious about having Robin come over to their house. "She worried about it a lot, so in the end I used to text him and tell him to come over because I thought he was a really cool guy."

Overall, however, Styles' adolescence was rather unremarkable, distinguished by the usual things teenagers go through as they navigate growing up. Despite his affable demeanour, he told *Rolling Stone* he "had a phase of listening to really heavy music. Not stupid heavy, but a bit ... just because I thought it was cool." His clothing rebellion was charmingly tame: it took the form of wearing black clothes and Nirvana T-shirts. Like many teens, he also had a job in order to pick up some extra spending money. Styles spent Saturday mornings behind the counter at W Mandeville bakery, helping customers while sporting a white-collared shirt and a striped maroon apron.

"He is a down-to-earth kid, and always has been"

Styles noted, after he no longer worked there, he did miss the baked goods he'd receive on his break. But he was still working at the bakery – and singing with White Eskimo – when he tried out for *The X Factor* in April 2010. "Winning the Battle of the Bands and playing to that many people really showed me that's what I wanted to do," he said in an interview for the show. "I got such a thrill when I was in front of people singing. It made me want to do more and more."

Styles seemed to audition for *The X Factor* for a bit of a lark. "I remember looking at the young guys on there – and I was kind of like, 'I'd love to have a go at it just to see what happens,' and that was kind of it," he later recalled to *Rolling Stone*, noting his mum actually filled out his application. At the time of his try-out, he was

LEFT One Direction launch their first single 'What Makes You Beautiful' in 2011.

OVERLEAF Harry travels in a luxury helicopter to Glasgow, Manchester and London, 2011.

LEFT Harry performs with One Direction at the televised BBC Children In Need Appeal, 2011.

equally blasé when telling the judges why he decided to audition, casually saying, "I've always wanted to audition but I've always been too young, so I thought I'd give it a whirl this time."

Styles chose to sing Train's 'Hey, Soul Sister' for his try-out. Although he looks quite earnest, and at one point flashes a dimple-heavy smile at the audience, his vocal delivery is sadly wavering and off-key. Cowell recognized that the music might have been affecting his concentration, and asked him to sing something a cappella. Styles chose Stevie Wonder's 'Isn't She Lovely' – and sounded markedly more self-assured.

Styles then faced a critique from Cowell and the other judges. "For 16 years old, you have a beautiful voice," Nicole Scherzinger told him. Louis Walsh was less enthusiastic, saying, "I agree with Nicole. However, I think you're so young, I don't think you have enough experience or confidence yet." Speaking in his usually direct way, Cowell sided with Scherzinger, observing, "I think with a bit of vocal coaching, you actually could be very good."

In the end, although Walsh voted not to let him move forward on the show – a decision that drew a loud chorus of boos from the crowd – the other two judges voted yes. Years later, Styles reminisced about what it felt like to go through this gauntlet. "In that instant, you're in the whirlwind," he told *Rolling Stone*. "You don't really know what's happening; you're just a kid on the show. You don't even know you're good at anything. I'd gone because my mum told me I was good from singing in the car ... but your mum tells you things to make you feel good, so you take it with a pinch of salt. I didn't really know what I was expecting when I went on there."

To be fair, nobody expected that Styles' time on *The X Factor* would become what it did – or possess a roller coaster's worth of unexpected twists and turns. But appearing on the show ended up changing his life – and kick-started a career that continues to go beyond even his wildest dreams.

CHAPTER 2

THIS IS US

PAGE 28 Harry Styles performs during *The X Factor* live show, 27 November 2010.

LEFT Harry attends the GQ Men of the Year Awards, 2011.

Redemption stories don't get much better than the origins of One Direction. The five members of the group – Harry Styles, Liam Payne, Louis Tomlinson, Niall Horan, and Zayn Malik – originally auditioned for the seventh season of *The X Factor* as soloists. Unfortunately, all five were on the brink of elimination, with Styles' shaky take on Oasis' 'Stop Crying Your Heart Out' putting his status in jeopardy.

However, fate intervened. During the bootcamp portion of the season, three of the show's judges (Simon Cowell, Nicole Scherzinger and Louis Walsh) decided to put together a boy band from the existing pool of contestants. The trio pored over Polaroids of these aspiring vocalists, intent on assembling a group that possessed an elusive "It factor". Scherzinger especially saw potential in the future members of One Direction, gushing first over the fact that Horan, Tomlinson and Styles looked good together. She observed, "You can't get rid of little stars – so you put them all together."

The judges settled on a boy band after adding Payne and Malik into the mix – and on 23 July 2010, One Direction was officially born. "This is a lifeline," judge Simon Cowell told the excited crew when they found out about their second chance. "You have got to work 10, 12, 14 hours a day, every single day, and take this opportunity. You've got a real shot here, guys."

As we all know now, that ended up being a vast understatement. Although One Direction inexplicably ended up finishing third on *The X Factor* – solo artists Matt Cardle and Rebecca Ferguson

PREVIOUS PAGES One Direction (L-R): Liam Payne, Louis Tomlinson, Harry Styles, Zayn Malik and Niall Horan.

ABOVE One Direction arrive for an autograph signing session at HMV in Bradford, UK.

landed in first and second place, respectively – they went on to sell millions of records and become one of the biggest, most beloved pop bands in the world. Reaching this status didn't come easy, of course; Cowell was correct in saying that achieving this kind of success requires hard work and dedication. And over the next few months, One Direction spent months refining their craft and figuring out how to be in a band.

It all started during the judges' house round in Marbella, Spain, where the newly minted group worked up two a cappella songs, Natalie Imbruglia's 'Torn' and Kelly Clarkson's 'My Life Would Suck Without You'. Styles took a prominent role in both choruses, belting out the lovelorn, anguished hook of 'Torn' and embracing his pop-star persona on Clarkson's tune. Cowell was satisfied enough with the performances to send One Direction into the next round. All of the boys were emotional, but Styles especially was overwhelmed (in a good way) with happy tears in light of the decision.

One Direction's meteoric rise started once *The X Factor*'s live episodes kicked off in October 2010; in fact, adoring screams echoed from the audience throughout the first episode, during which the group performed an up-tempo, almost Broadway-esque version of Coldplay's 'Viva La Vida'. Unfortunately, Styles' nerves reared their ugly head the week after and he felt ill, though he rallied as One Direction reprised their cover of 'My Life Would Suck Without You'. The upbeat version impressed Cowell, who said, "You are the most exciting pop band in the country today."

Wilson

"[Simon] Cowell was satisfied enough with the performances to send One Direction into the next round."

LEFT Harry signs autographs for fans in New York City, 2012.

By the third week, which found the group indulging their power ballad side with a soaring take on P!nk's 'Nobody Knows', One Direction hysteria was starting to take off. "It's like five Justin Biebers!" judge Walsh exclaimed after the performance, as the cheering crowd nearly drowned him out. Footage of the band going shopping resembled a small-scale Beatlemania, as they were greeted by flashing cameras and ecstatic fans; one excited teenage girl exclaimed repeatedly, "He winked at me!"

During the next few weeks, One Direction easily moved into the Top 10. They indulged their pop-rock side with an anthemic cover of Kim Wilde's new wave classic 'Kids in America' – which sounded tailor-made for the group – and showed off their burgeoning vocal maturity with a cover of Elton John's majestic anthem 'Something About the Way You Look Tonight'. The crowd response ramped up considerably when Styles launched into a solo; he responded with a poised performance.

Week after week, viewers tuned in as the group's self-assurance and chemistry grew – and One Direction continued to amass more and more fans. The group excelled when tackling rock songs, particularly a brisker, R'n'B-leaning arrangement of the Beatles' 'All You Need Is Love'. And Styles had a particularly good week when the group performed two classic tunes: the Joe Cocker-popularized 'You Are So Beautiful To Me' and Bryan Adams' 'Summer of '69'. The former suited Styles' range and demeanour, and as he poured his heart into the gorgeous song, the camera zoomed in for a close-up shot of his face. The golden-brown lighting and his tousled haircut made him resemble a 1970s teen heartthrob.

After the group's spirited version of 'Summer of '69', Cowell went out of his way to point out that Styles, who was wearing a Rolling Stones T-shirt, picked the song – a fitting but unsurprising choice, since he knew the tune quite well from his days fronting White Eskimo. However, the song choice also illustrated his quiet confidence as a leader; not only did Styles know his strengths as a vocalist, he was already working to amplify the strengths of One Direction.

At this point, however, tensions were high, as the group had made it to the final five acts of the show. But One Direction leapt into the finals with ease thanks to a fantastic production of Rihanna's 'Only Girl (In the World)' and a note-perfect version of Snow Patrol's aching 'Chasing Cars'. During the two-day finals event, they continued to steamroll forward with a take on Elton John's 'Your Song' – another tune perfectly suited to Styles – and a duet with fellow (one-time) boy band member Robbie Williams.

As *The X Factor* wound down, One Direction did an in-store signing at an HMV record shop and an outdoor live gig. Both events drew hundreds of supportive fans, who braved cold December weather to scream, cheer and yell for the group. There was clear momentum on One Direction's side going into the finals, but in a shocking turn of events, the group came in third for the season; they were eliminated after performing Natalie Imbruglia's 'Torn' on the second night of the finals. The quintet looked absolutely devastated, but gamely and politely congratulated the eventual runner-up, Rebecca Ferguson, and did a brief live chat after hearing the bad news.

Despite the setback, optimism shone through from their judge and mentor, Simon Cowell. "This is just the beginning for these boys," he said. Once again, this would prove to be a massive understatement. By late January 2011, One Direction had signed a huge record deal with Cowell's label, Syco Music, and were in the US laying the groundwork for a debut album with the producer RedOne, who had previously found major success with Lady Gaga. Not long after, the group took a break to release a book (*One Direction: Forever Young (Our Official X Factor Story)*) and perform on *The X Factor* Live Tour, and then resumed work on

RIGHT One Direction meet fans at HMV Oxford Circus, London, 2011.

LEFT The X Factor Live Tour, Wembley Arena, London, 2011.

their own music. Incredibly enough, Styles turned 17 years old in the midst of this whirlwind of activity.

As with many high-profile pop albums, One Direction's debut was a globe-spanning production. The group recorded in Los Angeles, London and Stockholm, and cut songs co-written by stars such as Ed Sheeran and Kelly Clarkson, as well as A-list songwriters Steve Robson (Rascal Flatts, Take That) and Toby Gad (Beyoncé, Fergie, Demi Lovato). *The X Factor*'s vocal coach, Savan Kotecha – who had also written hits for Usher and Britney Spears – co-wrote One Direction's official debut single, 'What Makes You Beautiful'. (A lovely cover of Alphaville's 'Forever Young' was slated to be One Direction's debut single had they won *The X Factor*; alas, it wasn't meant to be.)

Styles loved 'What Makes You Beautiful', Kotecha told *The Hollywood Reporter*. "When he heard the demo, I was in Miami, on my way back to Sweden, and he sent me a text message saying, 'I think you got it. I think you got the one here.'" In a subsequent MTV UK interview, Styles elaborated on what drew him to the song: "I think for us we wanted to release something that wasn't cheesy but it was fun. It kind of represented us, I think it took us a while to find it but I think we found the right song."

An airtight power-pop song that shows off the group's sparkling personalities and effervescent harmonies, 'What Makes You Beautiful' was indeed the perfect introduction to One Direction. Released on 10 August 2011, the single unsurprisingly went straight into the UK charts at No. 1 and eventually took home the 2012 Brit Award for British Single of the Year. Over time, it sold millions of copies around the world and became One Direction's signature song.

Styles still plays 'What Makes You Beautiful' in his solo shows, and it's easy to see why. For starters, he was lead vocals on the chorus, meaning he's the careful steward of the song's heartfelt expressions of love and desire. But 'What Makes You Beautiful' also captured the inclusive, positive vibe and ethos espoused by One Direction – and, by extension, Styles. If anything, the song served as a blueprint for his entire career.

In November, One Direction signed an American record deal with Columbia Records; in the UK and other parts of the world they also released their debut album, *Up All Night*. Although at

BRIT
AWARDS
2012
MasterCard
BRIT
AWARDS
2012
BRIT

BRIT
AWARDS
2012
MasterCard
BRIT
AWARDS
2012
MasterCard

PREVIOUS PAGES Harry Styles, Louis Tomlinson, Liam Payne, Zayn Malik and Niall Horan of One Direction pictured with their award for Best British Single, at the 2012 BRIT Awards.

RIGHT Harry and his 'I <3 Louis' shirt, 2011.

heart a collection of pop songs, the album also nods to classic rock, 1970s singer-songwriter fare, adult contemporary ballads and the polished anthems favoured by '90s boy bands. Styles had co-writing credits on several songs, including 'Taken' – on which he also shows off his tender vocal side, despite lyrics chiding someone who is only attracted to unavailable people – the dance-pop trifle 'Everything About You' and Keane-like 'Same Mistakes'.

Up All Night was a roaring success, debuting at No. 2 in the UK and spending seven weeks in the Top 10. Upon its March 2012 release in the US – merely weeks after Styles celebrated his 18th birthday – the album was an even bigger smash. It topped the *Billboard* 200 albums chart, making One Direction the first UK group to debut at No. 1 with their first album. 'What Makes You Beautiful' was also a success stateside. Bolstered by remixes by Dave Audé and Lenny B, the single reached No. 1 on the *Billboard* Dance Club Songs chart, and peaked at No. 4 on the *Billboard* Hot 100 singles chart.

When One Direction started doing promotion in the US, the response was as overwhelming (and positive) as it was in the UK. The day before *Up All Night*'s release, nearly 15,000 fans converged on New York City's Rockefeller Plaza bright and early in the morning for the group's national TV debut. One Direction made an appropriately grand entrance, travelling to the stage in an open-top double-decker bus emblazoned with their logo and then taking their places on49stage in front of their dapper-looking band. As it turns out, this feverish response was just a small taste of what was to come for One Direction in the future.

HARRY
LOUIS.

CHAPTER 3

BEST SONG EVER

PAGE 46 Harry Styles arrives at the American Music Awards, 2014.

LEFT Harry performs with One Direction at the BBC Radio 1 Teen Awards 2012 in London.

By early spring 2012, One Direction was a bona fide phenomenon. In the UK, the group had charted five singles, including three that reached the Top 10, and embarked on the sold-out *Up All Night* Tour. In America, One Direction had opened shows for fellow boy band Big Time Rush and announced headlining tour dates to promote their No. 1 album *Up All Night*. Unsurprisingly, the US leg of the *Up All Night* Tour was a hot ticket: the band's show at the legendary New York arena Madison Square Garden sold out in less than 10 minutes.

Understandably, all of these milestones meant that some people started comparing One Direction to the Beatles. Speaking to Larry London of VOA (Voice of America) that July, Styles modestly denied that parallel "If you base your career on trying to achieve someone else's goals, it is the wrong way to do it. We like to achieve things ourselves. We kind of find it a bit ridiculous because the Beatles are such an icon."

On the downside, One Direction's increased popularity meant that every move Styles made came under the microscope. Naturally, this scrutiny especially applied to his dating life, and he was linked to (or rumoured to be linked to) multiple celebrities. In an autumn 2012 interview with tabloid paper *The Mirror*, he addressed claims that he was a womanizer ("I don't like going crazy-crazy, I like having fun but it's nice to wake up in your own bed, isn't it?") and downplayed the wildness of his dating status: "I'm an 18-year-old boy and I'm having fun. I'm just not having as much fun as people make out."

Among other things, Styles was likely referring to his 2011 relationship with *The Xtra Factor* host and future *Love Island* UK host Caroline Flack, which drew heavy tabloid coverage. However, he was in the spotlight once again in late 2012 when he briefly dated Taylor Swift. The two notoriously shared a cosy date at Central Park Zoo, were spotted hand-in-hand in England and then kissed at midnight after she performed on *Dick Clark's New Year's Rockin' Eve with Ryan Seacrest*. By early 2013, however, things had cooled off between them after a vacation in the British Virgin Islands.

Time has softened any hurt feelings between the duo – in fact, they were spotted catching up at the Grammy Awards in 2021 and 2023. And Styles has been kind to his younger self when reminiscing about the Central Park date. "When I see photos from that day I think: relationships are hard, at any age," he told *Rolling Stone*. "And adding in that you don't really understand exactly how it works when you're 18, trying to navigate all that stuff didn't make it easier."

Still, none of these things detracted from the music or Styles' desire to make sure One Direction kept evolving. "It's good if you don't have a moment where you go, 'You know, I've made it', because

RIGHT Backstage at BBC's Children in Need, 16 November 2012.

ABOVE Harry Styles performs onstage with One Direction in front of fans at the Rockefeller Plaza, New York City, 2012.

I think it's important that you keep changing up your goals and stuff to make sure you don't kind of take your foot off the pedal," he told a reporter. "I think you have to keep making sure that you're always on top of your game."

That growth came to light on One Direction's second album, *Take Me Home*. Released in November 2012, the record featured many of the same songwriters that appeared on *Up All Night*, including Styles. He co-wrote the brisk pop gem 'Back For You' – a reassuring song where the narrator always comes back to their special someone – and the mellower, string-swept 'Summer Love'; the latter is a meditative, melancholy look back at an ephemeral love affair. For good measure, Styles also had a hand in writing two bonus tracks: the harmony-heavy, heart-on-sleeve ballad 'Irresistible' and the pop-punk-inspired plea for forgiveness 'Still the One'.

Preceded by the smash single 'Live While We're Young', *Take Me Home* sold 540,000 copies in the US during its first week on sale – triple the number *Up All Night* sold in week one – and easily reached No. 1 on the *Billboard* album charts. In the UK, both the album and the single 'Little Things' debuted at the top of their respective charts; One Direction were the youngest group ever to pull off this feat. Fittingly, they won Best International Artist at Australia's ARIA (Australian Recording Industry Association) Music Awards – the first of five straight wins in this category.

The group closed out the year on the road – a trek that included *two* appearances in one week at Madison Square Garden. After their long-sold-out headlining concert (which featured an epic cover of Wheatus' 2000 hit 'Teenage Dirtbag' and a surprise guest appearance from Ed Sheeran on 'Little Things', which Sheeran co-wrote), One Direction played a short set at the Z100 radio station-sponsored Jingle Ball just four days later. For the second year in a row, the quintet also acknowledged their roots and made a guest appearance on *The X Factor* UK live final.

As the calendar turned to 2013, things continued to go One Direction's way. The group booked a massive world tour, which started in February and continued into early November. They released a Comic Relief benefit song that mashed together Blondie's 'One Way or Another' and The Undertones' 'Teenage Kicks'. Called 'One Way or Another (Teenage Kicks)', the snappy, rock-orientated tune peaked at No. 1 in the UK and demonstrated the band's ever-expanding sound. At the 2013 American Music Awards, One Direction won Favorite Pop/Rock Album for *Take Me Home* and Pop/Rock Band/Duo/Group Award – and they also won the 2013 BRITs Global Success Award.

Buoyed by so much love, One Direction made moves to elevate their artistry. In July 2013, they released a new single, the effervescent power-pop tune 'Best Song Ever', which reached No. 2 on both the US and UK singles charts. The song came with a hilarious, Monkees-esque music video co-written by comedian James Corden. The clip mocks One Direction's burgeoning fame via a plot featuring out-of-touch industry executives – played by the band members themselves in disguise – attempting to sell the quintet on eye-roll-worthy movie ideas and outfits. Styles charmingly portrays a marketing guy named Marcel, envisioning the role as an earnest nerd who's trying (but failing) to impress his bosses and the group.

The single appeared on 2013's *Midnight Memories*, which once again topped the charts around the world and broke sales records. In the UK, *Midnight Memories* sold 237,000 copies in a week –

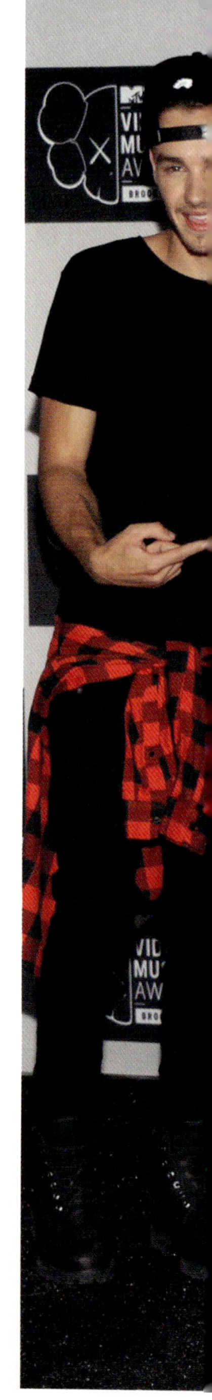

RIGHT At the MTV Video Music Awards, in Brooklyn, New York City, 2013.

LOVE WILL TEAR US APART

> **"Well, if I was going to write a song about myself, I'd probably never sing it."**

making it the fastest-selling album since a Michael Bublé Christmas album set charts ablaze in 2011 – while in America, the full-length sold a whopping 546,000 copies.

Styles had slightly more co-writes this time around, highlighted by the lovelorn ballad 'Story Of My Life', which reached No. 2 in the US and UK. The creative environment in which he wrote his *Midnight Memories* songs foreshadowed his solo career: he worked with small groups of songwriters that sometimes (and sometimes not) included members of One Direction. With OneRepublic ringleader Ryan Tedder, he wrote 'Right Now', a sweeping pop song about pining for someone far away; alongside producer Jacknife Lee and Snow Patrol's Gary Lightbody, he wrote the earnest 'Something Great'.

The indie-folk tune 'Happily' – in which a narrator pledges eternal fidelity as a way to coax someone to stay in a relationship – was even more important to Styles; in fact, it's not a stretch to say it was the pivotal point in his career. The song "was the first time I saw my name in the credits," he told *Rolling Stone* years later. "I liked that. But I knew I'd only sing part of it. I knew if I wrote a really personal song, I wouldn't sing it."

Styles described having other voices around him to handle these kinds of lyrics as "like a safety net." He added, "If a song was too personal, I could back away and say, 'Well, I don't have anything to do with it.' The writing was like, 'Well, if I was going to write a song about myself, I'd probably never sing it.'" But with the benefit of perspective, Styles understood that, as his songs evolved, he might

LEFT Harry arrives at the 2012 MTV Video Music Awards at the Staples Center, Los Angeles, 2012.

change his mind about performing such introspective material. "As the songs got more personal," he told *Rolling Stone*, "I think I just became more aware that at some point there might be a moment where I would want to sing it myself."

However, Styles wasn't quite ready for a solo career just yet. In 2014, One Direction booked their first stadium tour, the Where We Are Tour, which travelled to South America, Europe, the UK and North America. The time they spent on the road made a big difference, as the group demonstrated the kind of confidence that suited the larger venues; Styles in particular sported a longer hairstyle and all-black outfits that exuded rock 'n' roll swagger. Among the highlights of the tour was a three-night, sold-out stand at Wembley Stadium, an honour dampened somewhat by the fact that Styles developed tonsillitis. "I was miserable," he told *Rolling Stone* years later. "I remember I came off, got in the car, and just started crying because I was so disappointed."

RIGHT Niall Horan, Liam Payne, Harry Styles and Louis Tomlinson of One Direction perform live onstage, December 2015.

In between tour dates, One Direction found time to record and release another album, 2014's *Four*. It once again reached No. 1 around the world, including in the UK and US; in fact, One Direction became the first group ever to have their first four studio records debut at the top of the charts. Musically, the collection marked a turning point, as the group had writing credits on the bulk of the record.

"I just became more aware that at some point there might be a moment where I would want to sing it myself."

Styles especially had more of a hand in the recording process, co-writing the pensive UK Top 10 hit 'Night Changes' – which features a restless woman who feels lost but has a significant other offering grounding reassurance – and the equally stripped-down 'Fool's Gold', a song about falling for someone who's fake but irresistible. On the more upbeat side, Styles also co-wrote the galloping, mesmerized-by-romance tale 'Stockholm Syndrome' and the shout-from-the-rooftops pop tune 'Where Do Broken Hearts Go'; the latter features someone who's crushed the heart of a significant other and is trying (but not succeeding) to mend that fence.

Still, there were cracks in the successful facade. Zayn Malik left One Direction in March 2015, leaving the group to tour stadiums

Styles

LEFT Performing at the Jingle Ball in Los Angeles, 2015.

as a quartet on the forthcoming On the Road Again Tour. By this time, however, Styles was a seasoned enough performer to handle these bumps in the road, and he didn't necessarily feel too nervous performing live – although he admitted that it took a bit to get into the groove. "The fear of it has turned into adrenaline," he told *GQ* in 2015. "Definitely the first few shows you're scared as that's when all the mistakes happen. And then once you get your bearings and you know what you're doing you can enjoy it more."

Of course, even at the height of One Direction's popularity, Styles was quite unflappable and level-headed about fame – and firm about protecting his privacy. "I don't think you can ever get used to being this famous," he told *GQ*. "I've learned how to keep things separate or at a distance. I've nothing to hide. But seeing this as work, like a job, means I can take a step back. It's me right now in front of you and in the papers – but it's not all of me."

This attitude was rooted in self-preservation and personal experience, as One Direction's booming career meant the unassuming kid from Holmes Chapel was now a global superstar. But even as the group achieved milestones like stadium tours and multiple number one albums, Styles was starting to think about his own future – and what was next.

CHAPTER 4

SIGN OF THE TIMES

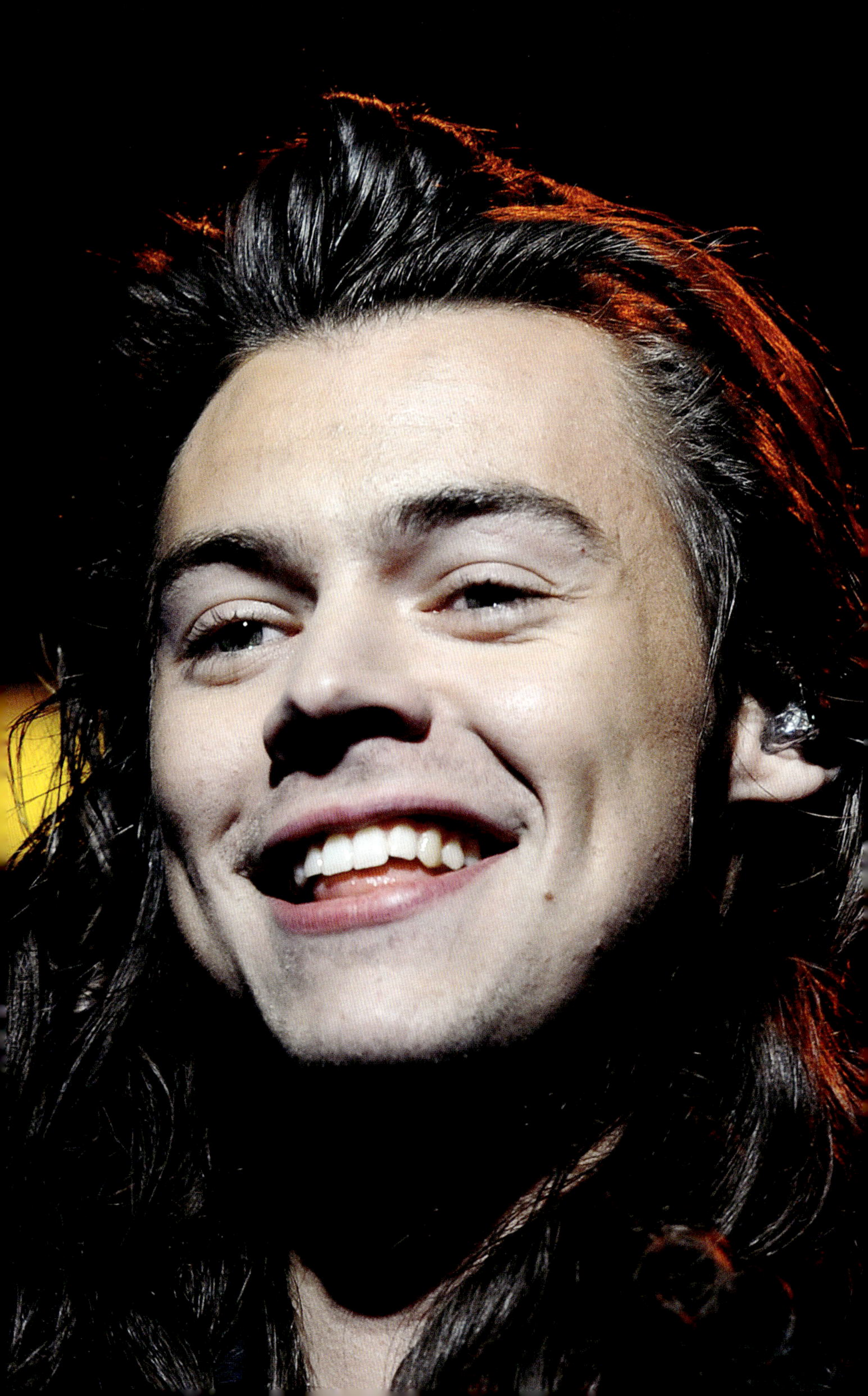

PAGE 62 Performing live onstage during Harry Styles: Live On Tour, Madison Square Garden, 21 June 2018 in New York City.

OPPOSITE Harry Styles, 2015.

August 2015 brought some incredibly distressing news for One Direction fans: the group appeared to be on the verge of breaking up. Niall Horan took to social media to offer some reassuring words, clarifying that One Direction were taking a "well-earned break at some point next year." But it soon became clear that this break might be more permanent than people were letting on. For starters, the band had planned out this time off in advance. In an interview with *Billboard*, songwriter-producer Julian Bunetta said that the possibility of a break loomed over the recording sessions for One Direction's forthcoming fifth studio album, *Made in the A.M.*. "There was definitely a vibe of making [the album] the best it can possibly be," he said, "and knowing it has to last as long as it needs to until we make another record – if we make another record."
If that comment wasn't ominous enough, UK tabloids also started reporting rumours that Sony Music was angling to sign Styles to a solo record deal. Representatives issued swift denials – and, for the rest of 2015, One Direction embarked on what amounted to something between a victory lap and a long farewell. The group booked a summer US stadium tour, followed up with more concerts in the UK and Ireland, and then made the rounds of high-profile radio festivals and TV shows. They also continued racking up honours, such as their second straight Artist of the Year win at the American Music Awards.

In November, One Direction also released *Made in the A.M.*. Like their other albums, it was a global success, reaching No. 1 (or at least coming close to that peak) around the world. Styles co-wrote

The possibility of a break loomed over the recording sessions for One Direction's fifth studio album, *Made in the A.M.*.

several of its tracks, which in hindsight foreshadowed the musical directions he would explore as a solo artist. These songs included the tender, string-swept piano ballad 'If I Could Fly' – during which Styles showed off a smoky tone, while taking a solo turn on the first verse and chorus – and 'Olivia', a psychedelic-pop gem bolstered with a whimsical full orchestra recorded at Abbey Road Studios.

Bunetta told *Rolling Stone* that 'Olivia' represented "Harry's genius", as the Beatles-esque song arrived in a burst of inspiration after a few days of writer's block. "At the very end of the day when Harry was going to leave, he was sort of saying the chorus phrase, so we just sat there and wrote it really quick," he said. "... That was an incredibly adult, musically indulgent song that we all had a lot of fun making."

Styles' third co-write – the midtempo pop-rock ballad 'Perfect' – was also quite sophisticated, although lyrically it's a rather mischievous ode to a no-strings-attached romance. Some suspected the song was about his short-lived relationship with Taylor Swift, although Styles demurred on specifics. "I think people interpret songs in different ways," he told *People*. "I'm never going to tell someone what a song's about because I feel like it's up to them."

'Perfect' ended up becoming One Direction's second-to-last chart hit, and one of the songs the group performed at their last live appearance to date: closing out 2015 on the annual TV special *Dick Clark's New Year's Rockin' Eve with Ryan Seacrest*. That same week, Internet sleuths dug up more evidence of a burgeoning Styles solo career: four compositions in a song publishing database registered with him listed as the performer.

Soon it was 2016 and the dust settled on One Direction's hiatus, whispers that Styles would be branching out on his own grew

BELOW Members of One Direction perform on ABC's *Good Morning America*, 2015.

CASAMIGOS

LEFT Styles attends the 2018 Casamigos Halloween Party, California, dressed as Elton John.

louder. A few months later, those long-gestating rumours came true: the musician signed a high-profile management deal in March and then, a few months later, formed his own independent record label, Erskine Records. That was followed by inking a solo deal with Columbia Records, the major label that had released One Direction's albums.

Speaking to *Rolling Stone*, Styles stressed how much he cherished One Direction and the group's integrity – "I love the band, and would never rule out anything in the future. The band changed my life, gave me everything" – but was also clear about why it was so important for him to go solo. "I wanted to step up," he said. "There were songs I wanted to write and record, and not just have it be 'Here's a demo I wrote.'" Styles added that he also wanted more say over his own destiny – and career direction. "Every decision I've made since I was 16 was made in a democracy. I felt like it was time to make a decision about the future ... and maybe I shouldn't rely on others."

To that end, Styles set up a business deal where he would technically license his music to Columbia via Erskine Records – thereby giving him more control and ownership over his solo records. And he also knew that he needed the right collaborators to make his vision a reality. Enter Jeff Bhasker, who had previously worked with rapper Kanye West, electro-funk maestro Mark Ronson and the rock band fun. All of these artists found pop success with striking original music, making Bhasker a perfect choice to be executive producer as Styles found his solo sound.

On the production side, Styles also assembled a crew of like-minded collaborators. In addition to Bhasker, he worked with producers Alex Salibian, Tyler Johnson and Kid Harpoon. Their backgrounds tended to include creative partnerships with artists who disliked being pigeonholed. Johnson received a Grammy nomination for his engineering work on Taylor Swift's *Red* – an album known for blurring the lines between pop, rock and country – and also co-wrote the folk-rock hit 'Burning House' by the country artist Cam, while Salibian worked with iconoclastic solo acts such as Mikky Ekko and Elle King. Kid Harpoon, meanwhile, had credits on Florence & the Machine's anthemic hits 'Shake It Out' and 'Never Let Me Go' – and had dabbled in writing with Styles before. "I just remember thinking, 'Man, when he does his album, I want to be there because this guy is special," he later told *Billboard*.

Bhasker and his team also used their connections to help Styles put together a band for the recording sessions, another crucial step in the creative process. Among the musicians they recruited was a jazz-loving guitarist and drummer named Mitch Rowland, who quickly became a trusted writing partner *and* touring band member. "He was working in a pizza shop and had never been in a studio," Styles said in the documentary *Harry Styles: Behind the Album*. "It felt like we kind of had each other ... [it helped to] have someone who had no preconceived notions about me or who I was or anything."

With this new crew in place, Styles didn't rush his creativity *or* inspiration. He took his time putting the album together, travelling to familiar places, such as England and California, as well as new locales. In the autumn of 2016, Styles spent two months working on music in Jamaica at Geejam Studios, a secluded studio near Port Antonio. "It felt like a little secret," he said in *Behind the Album*. "It's fun to feel like no one knows where you are. It made such a difference from being in a busy city. It created this, like, total 360[-degree] writing experience that I've never had before."

"It's fun to feel like no one knows where you are. It made such a difference from being in a busy city."

The focused, extended sessions that took place in Jamaica were a luxury, especially compared to the compressed timelines under which One Direction worked. And the lack of a public microscope was a boon for his creativity: Styles and his collaborators wrote six songs that ended up on the album a short time after arriving. The pressure-free environment helped Styles open up and write about his own life experiences.

For example, certain songs reportedly drew on his relationship with model and reality star Kendall Jenner. Rumours that the pair were dating began when Styles was still in One Direction, and crested around the start of 2016, when the couple were spotted hanging out together on yachts. Years later, even Jenner was curious about Styles' creative inspirations. "I'm dying to know this: which songs on your last album were about me?" she asked him in December 2019, when the pair appeared together on *The Late Late*

RIGHT Harry Styles performing at the Miller Park Stadium during the On the Road Again tour, Milwaukee, Wisconsin, 2015.

PREVIOUS PAGES Harry Styles performs on NBC's *Today* show at Rockefeller Center, New York City, 9 May 2017.

RIGHT Zayn Malik, 2015

Show with James Corden and played the truth-or-dare-like game, "Fill Your Guts or Spill Your Guts". Styles was so against revealing specifics, he chose to take the dare and eat cod sperm instead.

For Styles, being so deliberate and thoughtful about his solo debut was important. He was trying to figure out what he wanted to sound like – and, musically, who he wanted to be – outside of One Direction. Being true to himself while finding his solo voice was also absolutely crucial. "I think it was tough to really delve in and find out who you are as a writer when you're just kind of dipping your toe each time," he told *Rolling Stone,* referencing his One Direction days. "We didn't get the six months to see what kind of shit you can work with. To have time to live with a song, see what you love as a fan, chip at it, hone it and go for that ... it's heaven."

Technically, Styles wasn't the first member of One Direction to go solo and find his niche. That honour went to Zayn Malik, who departed the group in 2015 and enjoyed chart-topping success the following year with both a single ('Pillowtalk') and an album (*Mind of Mine*). Malik dug deep into contemporary pop and R'n'B, which suited his voice perfectly and made the transition to a solo career easy. Styles, however, was determined to follow his muse – even if it pulled him in against-the-grain directions that weren't necessarily contemporary.

By late March 2017, Styles was ready to pull back the curtain and show the world what he had been working on, and released an enigmatic teaser video. As haunting piano music plays in the background, he walks through clouds of smoke toward a door that's

LEFT Harry sporting a paisley suit during a performance in Sydney, Australia, 2017.

slightly ajar. Styles then fully opens the door, letting a beam of light shine through so he's seen in silhouette. After a brief close-up of his eyes, a date flashes on the screen: April 7.

That ended up being the premiere day of his debut solo single, 'Sign of the Times'. Calling it "the song I'm most proud of writing" on the BBC's *Radio 1 Breakfast Show*, he compared the release experience to a lengthy gestation: "I feel like I've been hibernating for so long ... and now it's time to give birth." To no one's surprise, the song went straight into the UK singles charts at No. 1, and spent seven weeks overall in the Official Charts Top 10. In the US, 'Sign of the Times' debuted at No. 4 on the *Billboard* Hot 100. Styles was on his way to solo stardom.

A week after releasing his debut single, Styles was the musical guest on *Saturday Night Live*. He performed not just 'Sign of the Times', but another new tune, 'Ever Since New York'. He also stretched his acting skills in several skits, highlighted by an exaggerated (but hilarious) Mick Jagger impression in a skit involving the US TV game show *Family Feud*.

A month later came the music video for 'Sign of the Times'. It was a stunning and cinematic clip: Styles, clad in a long navy blue coat, wanders around the Isle of Skye in Scotland, looking a bit lost, until he steps off a rock and suddenly rises into the air as if an unseen force lifts him upward. This kicks off a panoramic trip that finds Styles flying over picturesque forests, gorgeous waterfalls and a body of water with a rippling whirlpool, before ending the journey by ascending into puffy clouds and a brilliant sunset.

The video and single release set the stage for the May release of the album *Harry Styles*, which was another immediate hit. Buoyed by several high-profile promotional appearances – a week-long residency on *The Late Late Show with James Corden* and a performance in New York City's Rockefeller Plaza, where fans slept outside overnight for days to get the best viewing spot – the album topped the charts in multiple countries around the world, including Australia, the US, the UK, Ireland and Canada. Styles undoubtedly now had a firm toehold as a solo artist.

The day after *Harry Styles* hit the stores, he announced a last-minute show at London venue The Garage – his first-ever official solo concert. Sporting the crisp pink suit he favoured during this era, Styles greeted the crowd politely – "Hello, London. I'm Harry; nice to meet you" – and ran through a set of songs from *Harry Styles*. However, he also covered Kanye West's 'Ultralight Beam' and strapped on a guitar to perform One Direction's 'Stockholm Syndrome'.

Styles' friend Stevie Nicks told *Vogue* that she was proud he achieved so much on his own terms. "Harry could've lost a lot of fans, but he didn't. I'm so proud of him because he took a risk and didn't go the One Direction route. He loves One Direction, I love One Direction, and a gazillion other people do too, but Harry didn't wanna go the pop route. He wanted straight-up rock and roll circa 1975." Fittingly, for Styles' debut American solo show at iconic Los Angeles club The Troubadour, Nicks was on hand to provide moral support and musical good vibes. She also performed three songs with him, including a cover of her Don Henley duet 'Leather and Lace'.

During this time, Styles also took on his first movie acting role, portraying a soldier named Alex in Christopher Nolan's 2017 World War II-era thriller-drama *Dunkirk*, alongside co-stars such as (among others) Kenneth Branagh, Mark Rylance, and Cillian Murphy. Despite already being a music star, he earned the gig just like any other actor, Nolan said: "Harry sent in a tape, and we liked the tape. And he joined the workshop, and that was that." *Dunkirk* was a massive success, grossing US$527 million worldwide. In December 2017, Styles also filled in as host for *The Late Late Show with James Corden* at the last minute, as Corden's wife went into hospital to have a baby girl.

ABOVE With One Direction at the American Music Awards in 2015. Harry's bold Gucci suit turns heads and marks the start of his fashion journey.

LEFT Harry attends the Victoria's Secret Fashion Show In Shanghai, 2017.

When Styles launched a global tour in early autumn 2017 – titled, simply, Harry Styles: Live on Tour – he continued to put a dividing line between One Direction and his solo work. Although he added a few old songs to his setlist (including, at various times, the One Direction tunes 'If I Could Fly', 'Story of My Life' and 'What Makes You Beautiful') he also performed a tune he wrote for Ariana Grande ('Just A Little Bit of Your Heart') and cover songs – for example, a stripped-down version of Little Big Town's 'Girl Crush' and a barn-burning take on Fleetwood Mac's 'The Chain'.

On special occasions, Styles also performed a few unique songs. At a June 2018 concert at Madison Square Garden, Kacey Musgraves joined him onstage for a languid cover of Shania Twain's 'You're Still The One'. Strumming an acoustic guitar, he belted out the second verse in a tender voice, and harmonized perfectly with Musgraves on the chorus. In Australia, meanwhile, he sang snippets of Rickie Lee Jones' 'The Horses', a nod to the fact that the Australian icon Daryl Braithwaite had a massive hit with his version of the song in 1991.

On this tour, Styles also debuted the non-album track 'Medicine', which immediately became a fan favourite. Musically, the song's galloping grooves and jagged electric guitar riffs echo '70s glam rock; thematically, 'Medicine' also nods to glam's fluid sexuality – the song's lyrics reference hooking up with a guy and winkingly describe sex as having the restorative power of medicine.

"I really love the song," Styles told Howard Stern. "I think I get kind of in my head [when] there's a song that didn't make an album before, I'm kind of like, 'Well, if it didn't make that one why would it make this one?' It feels older to me and I just feel better about the stuff that we're making in terms of what we're gonna put out now."

That relentless push forward – coupled with a remarkable ability to avoid being overly sentimental about the past – is indicative of Styles' solo career. But it's also one reason why he became so successful, so fast. He's always honoured his past music and achievements – but has never let them overshadow whatever he's doing in the present.

Fashion

LEFT Arriving for the premiere of *My Policeman* at the 2022 Toronto International Film Festival.

Styles never passes up an opportunity to rock an eye-catching outfit – or do fancy dress. His looks might include bright, patterned jumpsuits cut to show off his tattoos, tailored trousers with a decided '70s flair, a Gucci suit, or even a dress or kilt. As a co-host of the 2019 Met Gala – alongside fellow music icon Lady Gaga, tennis superstar Serena Williams, *Vogue* editor Anna Wintour and then-Gucci collaborator Alessandro Michele – Styles wore a black sheer blouse with frilly accents, high-waisted black pants, low-heeled black dress boots and a pearl earring. In a sign of his commitment to the outfit, he even pierced his ear specifically for the occasion.

Stylist Harry Lambert told *Vogue* that Styles' Met Gala look was "elegant" and "camp, but still Harry", as well as being a departure from his onstage attire. "This look is about taking traditionally feminine elements like the frills, heeled boots, sheer fabric and the pearl earring, but then rephrasing them as masculine pieces set against the high-waisted tailored trousers and his tattoos."

For the Met Gala after-party, Styles deliberately channelled another notable pop era: the early 1980s New Romantic movement popularized by bands such as Duran Duran and Spandau Ballet – he paired the high-waisted black trousers with a puffy white blouse and gigantic red bow, as well as a large cross earring.

Styles is also known for mixing and matching interesting pieces or colours. At the 2020 Brit Awards, he paired a bright yellow Marc Jacobs suit with a lilac blouse, while past looks have included the following: a Gucci brown mohair suit with dragon appliqué work, a purple iridescent Alexander McQueen suit and a sweater vest with a sheep pattern. Accessories-wise, Styles is known for statement necklaces – ones with pearls or chunky beads – as well as multi-hued nail polish, retro sunglasses, and colourful feather boas. And at the 2023 Brit Awards, Styles walked the red carpet wearing custom Nina Ricci by Harris Reed, in the form of a black tailored suit and a gigantic black satin organza oversized flower cushioning his neck.

"What women wear. What men wear. For me it's not a question of that," Styles told *The Guardian* in 2019. "If I see a nice shirt and get told, 'But it's for ladies.' I think: 'Okaaaay? Doesn't make me want to wear it less, though.' I think the moment you feel more comfortable with yourself, it all becomes a lot easier."

ABOVE The famous Gucci jacket and dress worn by Harry Styles for his 2020 *Vogue* cover.

RIGHT At the 2023 Annual Grammy Awards wearing a custom, rainbow-coloured, patterned jumpsuit by EgonLab in collaboration with Swarovski.

OVERLEAF Serena Williams, Harry Styles, Alessandro Michele, Lady Gaga and Anna Wintour at the 2019 Met Gala in New York City.

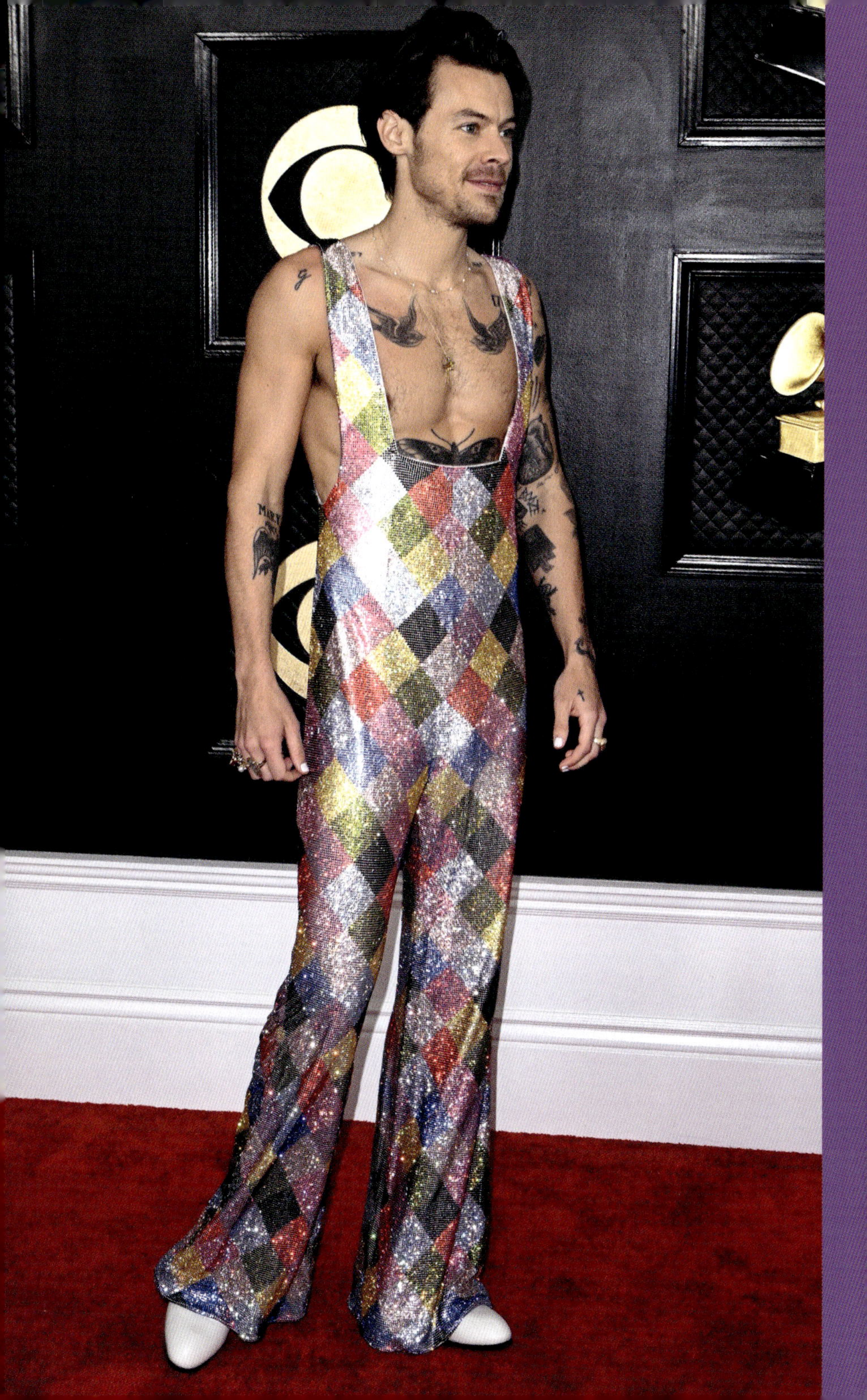

LG

CHAPTER 5

LIGHTS UP

PAGE 88 Celebrating the launch of *Fine Line* at a private listening session for fans, 11 December 2019, Los Angeles, California.

LEFT Harry Styles onstage at the O2 arena in London, December 2019.

With the 2017 release of his self-titled debut, Harry Styles successfully distinguished himself as a solo artist outside of One Direction. The album topped the charts around the globe and enabled Styles to embark on a well-received worldwide tour. Momentum *and* goodwill were on his side.

However, Styles felt a bit stressed as his second album, *Fine Line,* started coming together. "I felt like it had to be big," he told NPR (National Public Radio). "The last record wasn't really a radio record: the single ['Sign of the Times'] from it was a six-minute piano ballad, so it wasn't the typical formula. So I felt a bit of pressure that I wanted to make something that worked." Complicating matters further, Styles added that feeling pressured actually *didn't* help him write the songs he wanted. "That's when I make the music that I like the least – when I'm trying to write a pop song or I'm trying to write something fun."

As with his debut, however, Styles took his time finding his way forward for *Fine Line* – and relied on his collaborators for support. He reunited with Tyler Johnson and Kid Harpoon, both of whom had also appeared on *Harry Styles*, and let their collaborations unfold organically. They didn't book a series of regimented recording sessions in order to churn out a whole batch of potential songs. Instead, *Fine Line* was "made with a bunch of friends getting into the studio to see what happens," Kid Harpoon told *MusicWeek*. As it turns out, this collaborative chemistry made getting into a creative groove easier. "A lot of the best songs that came out weren't by anyone in particular," he added. "Harry was driving the vision, but the input came from everyone."

PREVIOUS PAGES At the 2020 BRIT Awards in London. Pictured is Jack Whitehall, Lizzo and Harry Styles.

RIGHT Harry performing at the BRIT Awards, London, 2020.

A great example of this is 'Cherry', which Styles said emerged in the wee hours of the morning. He was hanging out with Johnson and collaborator Sammy Witte, drinking tequila and waxing philosophical about the future. "I was saying how I have all these records that I'd love to make, I love all this kind of music and in five years I want to make *this* kind of record, and in 10 years I want to make *this* kind of album, and then I'll get to make the music that I really want to make," Styles told NPR. "And Tyler just said, 'You just have to make the music that you want to make – right now. That's the only way of doing it, otherwise you're going to regret it.'" That reality check woke Styles right up – and the crew ended up tracking 'Cherry' that very night.

Other songs came together just as spontaneously. Kid Harpoon revealed that 'Falling' emerged from an impromptu recording session. He had dropped by Styles' house to give him a ride somewhere, and as he waited for the musician to get ready after a shower, he played around on the piano. Styles started singing along and 'Falling' was done an hour later. He didn't even stop to get dressed, as he confessed to *Rolling Stone*: "I was completely naked when I wrote that song."

Both of these songs happen to be about the aftermath of his low-key romantic relationship with the model Camille Rowe. (That's even her speaking French at the start and end of 'Cherry', a slightly petulant song that obviously comes from a place of deep hurt.) Styles and Rowe dated for roughly a year from mid-2017 to summer

2018, and by all accounts their break-up affected Styles while making *Fine Line*.

For example, on 'Falling', he holds the mirror up to himself and his actions – there's a reference to him acting out of line due to drinking – and isn't quite sure he likes what he sees in the reflection. Still, *Fine Line* is far from a brooding break-up record. The breezy 'Watermelon Sugar' coalesced during what Kid Harpoon called a "catch up" in a Nashville recording studio while Styles was on tour. Much later, Styles revealed the song's meaning from the stage of a show, mischievously noting it's about "the sweetness of life", before adding, "It's also about the female orgasm, but that's totally different. It's not really relevant."

This open-minded attitude also had something to do with where Styles recorded. Among other places, he decamped to Malibu, California's Shangri-La studio, a place owned by the producer Rick Rubin. That studio was conducive to loosening up – Styles described things like 10 a.m. frozen margaritas and chocolate edibles chilling in a fridge – and expanding your mind. "We'd do mushrooms, lie down on the grass, and listen to Paul McCartney's *Ram* in the sunshine," he told *Rolling Stone*. "We'd just turn the speakers into the yard."

Such an idyllic atmosphere helped Styles get in the proper headspace to make a different record, one that sounded ebullient and lighter, despite its sometimes weighty source material. Styles told Zane Lowe how he felt "so much more joyous" this time around. "And I was with my friends and we were in Malibu ... I felt so safe. It was like, 'I want to take some mushrooms? I'm going to take some – like now is the time to have fun.'"

Fine Line's first single, 'Lights Up', is a marked evolution from the sound of Styles' debut album. The song boasts a chilled-out R'n'B groove with stuttering beats; a chorus with Bowie-circa-

RIGHT Performing 'Watermelon Sugar' onstage at the 2021 Grammy Awards, wearing a custom-made Gucci black leather suit and green feather boa.

novation

LEFT Harry waves a Pride flag during his performance at the Music Hall of Williamsburg, New York City.

Aladdin Sane piano and a twisting, minor-key melody; and a bridge with gospel-tinged vocal catharsis. In an interview with Capital FM, Styles described the song as being about "freedom and, I guess, self-reflection, self-discovery ... I guess a couple of things that I'd kind of thought about and, I guess, wrestled with a little bit over the last couple of years and then, I think, the song's kind of about me just accepting those things."

The music video for 'Lights Up' embodied those ideas. Throughout the clip, Styles is shirtless and glistening with sweat while dancing and writhing with a group of people spanning all genders, ostensibly at a party. At other points in the video, he rides on the back of a scooter, his arms out like he's flying; looks at himself in the mirror as if he's peering at a stranger; and is shown both standing and floating in a body of water. The imagery and moody lighting within these scenes call to mind heaven, hell and purgatory – a canny commentary on worrying about the consequences of your actions – but also seems to depict Styles going through a baptismal rebirth or coming into the light; both are a figurative way of looking at self-discovery.

Many fans noticed that the 'Lights Up' video premiere happened to coincide with on National Coming Out Day – 11 October – and wondered if that was Styles himself coming out or at least subtly sending a message about his sexuality. This chatter was nothing new: since the start of his career, Styles has been asked about his sexuality – sometimes rather directly.

For example, upon the release of his debut album, a journalist for *The Sun* brought up sexuality in pop music. "Everyone should just be who they want to be," Styles replied. "It's tough to justify somebody having to answer to someone else about stuff like that." The interviewer then asked if Styles had "personally labelled his sexuality," to which he replied he hadn't, saying, "I've never felt the need to really." Styles went on to affirm, "I don't feel like it's something I've ever felt like I have to explain about myself."

Indeed, Styles has been a long-time vocal ally for the queer community. Starting with his initial solo tours, he took to waving various flags (for example, the rainbow pride flag or trans flag) during shows as a sign of solidarity. During the *Fine Line* era, the conversation around Styles' sexuality coincidentally started buzzing again thanks to the album's striking cover art, which happened to

Styles has been a long-time vocal ally for the queer community.

use the bisexual pride colours (pink, purple and blue) and featured Styles sporting a magenta blouse.

The palette and his outfit didn't escape the notice of fans – and some people wondered about the optics of an ostensibly cisgender straight man using LGBTQ-associated imagery. Styles addressed the question honestly in a 2019 profile in *The Guardian*: "Am I sprinkling in nuggets of sexual ambiguity to try and be more interesting? No," he said, while adding, "In terms of how I wanna dress, and what the album sleeve's gonna be, I tend to make decisions in terms of collaborators I want to work with. I want things to look a certain way. Not because it makes me look gay, or it makes me look straight, or it makes me look bisexual, but because I think it looks cool."

In a 2022 *Better Homes & Gardens* interview, he used the term "outdated" to describe demands to define sexuality into a neat box. "I've been really open with it with my friends, but that's my personal experience; it's mine," he said. "The whole point of where we should be heading, which is toward accepting everybody and being more open, is that it doesn't matter, and it's about not having to label everything, not having to clarify what boxes you're checking."

This dislike of labels certainly extends to the trend-defying music Styles was making circa *Fine Line*. And by not being concerned about how his music was perceived – or how *he* was perceived – Styles opened himself up to even more success. 'Lights Up' reached No. 17 on the *Billboard* Hot 100, but peaked at No. 3 in the UK, setting the stage for even greater things to come.

RIGHT Harry Styles attends the BRIT Awards 2020 at the O2 arena in London in February 2020.

HOW
THE 4TH SH
RIT
ARDS
BR
AWA
2020
RITs

Leading up to the release of *Fine Line*, Styles didn't embark on a tour right away, although he did support the album with multiple appearances and performances. On 16 November 2019, Styles returned to *Saturday Night Live* and debuted the live versions of 'Lights Up' and 'Watermelon Sugar'. The former sounded like a cross between a solemn hymn and torch song. Sporting a glittery plum suit and hot pink nail polish, Styles crooned 'Lights Up' accompanied by a pianist, guitarist, three backing vocalists and, later, a trumpet player. 'Watermelon Sugar' was more upbeat and funky, thanks to a full horn section and a breezy, tropical-getaway groove. Fittingly, Styles almost looked like the juicy fruit, as he rocked a suit with a red shirt and pinkish jacket and trousers.

This appearance presaged a mysterious promotional push: travel-style advertisements for a quaint seaside town named Eroda, complete with a website (visiteroda.com) and picturesque photos. Fans soon figured out it had to do with Styles, thanks to Easter eggs on the website. The main clue was Eroda spelled backwards is Adore, referencing the track 'Adore You', and a line on the website said "we adore you". The "Attractions" listing on the page included Cherry Street and Golden Way – two tracks on the album were 'Cherry' and 'Golden'.

The end result was a music video for a new single, 'Adore You', with Scotland-filmed scenery standing in for the fictional village of Eroda.

The premise was adorable: Styles finds a golden fish in the ocean and takes it home to care for it. Bizarrely, however, the fish becomes very big, very fast – outgrowing a water jug, then a clear backpack and, eventually, even a gigantic aquarium tank. Along the way, he and Styles bond – the adoration hinted at in the song reflects their relationship – which leads to some silly moments: for example, at one point both Styles and his fishy friend are both pictured busting out some dance moves to the laid-back grooves of 'Adore You'. In the end, however, it becomes clear that the kindest thing Styles can

LEFT Kacey Musgraves and Harry Styles perform onstage at Bridgestone Arena in Nashville, 2019.

OVERLEAF Live onstage during the 2021 Grammy Awards.

do for the fish is to let it live in the ocean, where it'll be able to swim unencumbered.

A week after the 'Adore You' video premiered, *Fine Line* landed in stores. Styles celebrated the occasion with a special show at the Los Angeles Forum and another at the Electric Ballroom in London. In early 2020, he continued making the promo rounds, including a memorable March appearance on *The Howard Stern Show*, during which he and his band performed a smoking cover of Peter Gabriel's 'Sledgehammer'; Styles in particular showed off a soulful vocal delivery that was quite Gabriel-esque.

Unfortunately, the Covid-19 pandemic, which started in March 2020, halted some of Styles' *Fine Line* promotional plans; most notably, he had to postpone his intended tour dates. However, not even a lockdown could stop his commercial surge. In the UK, five singles from *Fine Line* reached the Top 40. Over in America, 'Adore You' was also a hit, peaking at No. 6, although Styles' biggest achievement was yet to come. During summer 2020, 'Watermelon Sugar' became his first *Billboard* Hot 100 No. 1 hit in America, reaching that peak for a week in August.

Styles continued making headlines later in the year when he became the first man ever to appear by himself on the cover of *Vogue*. His outfit of choice was a ruffled light blue Gucci dress with black accents and a black blazer. "Clothes are there to have fun with and experiment with and play with," Styles said in the accompanying cover story. "What's really exciting is that all of these lines are just kind of crumbling away. When you take away 'There's clothes for men and there's clothes for women', once you remove any barriers, obviously you open up the arena in which you can play."

The choice of outfits provoked discussion and debate, with the magazine *Dazed* publishing an article, "Just how revolutionary is Harry Styles' *Vogue* cover?" that explored the ins and outs of the fashion decision. Still, Styles was undeterred, and continued embracing unexpected fashion choices. In a winter 2021 *Dazed*

RIGHT Harry accepts the Grammy for Best Pop Solo Performance for 'Watermelon Sugar' in Los Angeles, 2021.

magazine cover feature, Styles' looks were playful and unexpected, conjuring things like whimsical *Alice in Wonderland* figures, the bewitching vibe of Stevie Nicks, and Shakespearean characters.

And at the 2021 Grammy Awards, when he performed a dynamite new arrangement of 'Watermelon Sugar' – transforming it into a 1970s soul-funk seduction, complete with a horn section and backing vocalists – his outfit suited the vibe: he draped a sea-green feather boa over a custom black leather Gucci suit with no shirt underneath. Styles followed up this look with another colourful outfit from the fashion brand: a lavender feather boa over a plaid yellow suit coat, a striped sweater and chocolate-brown corduroy pants.

LEFT Posing at the 2021 Grammys.

"Clothes are there to have fun with and experiment with and play with."

That the latter outfit resembled one worn by Cher Horowitz – the fashionable main character in the 1995 movie *Clueless* – caught the eye of Alicia Silverstone, who portrayed the iconic Cher. "I am loving the *Clueless* vibes, Harry Styles!!" Silverstone tweeted. "Cher would be so honored (and totally approve!!) of this chic look."

That same night, Styles won his first Grammy Award, taking home Best Pop Solo Performance for 'Watermelon Sugar'. Clearly nervous and maybe a little in awe of the honour, Styles made a very humble acceptance speech in which he thanked his collaborators, co-writers, label and manager, before ending by giving kudos to his peers. "I feel very grateful to be here," he concluded. "All of these songs [in the category] are fucking massive, so thank you so much. I feel very honoured to be among all of you."

At the time, little did Styles know that this award was just the beginning of another major career surge – one that would lead to bigger hits, bigger tours and the kind of ubiquitous stardom achieved by only very few musicians. In the moment, he was just soaking up the admiration for *Fine Line* – and enjoying the sweet rewards of success.

Stevie Nicks Friendship

They say you should never meet your idols. Luckily, Harry Styles didn't listen to that advice and actually did seek out and later befriend a legend he had long admired: Stevie Nicks, who found fame both with the band Fleetwood Mac and as a solo artist.

Styles first met Nicks backstage at a Fleetwood Mac show. As a token of his appreciation, he brought her a gift: delicious, personalized carrot cake. "Piped her name onto it," he told *Rolling Stone*. "She loved it. Glad she liked carrot cake." The sweet treat was the beginning of a beautiful friendship that's led to live collaborations and deep creative mentorship.

Styles grew up listening to Fleetwood Mac, so he later admitted that becoming pals with Nicks was somewhat mind-blowing. "I'm trying to enjoy being with her and soaking it in," he told NPR about being in the icon's orbit. "But I think at the same time, while you're in the room with her, I'm sitting there thinking about being ten years old and singing [Fleetwood Mac's 'Dreams']."

However, the respect is mutual. "Harry writes and sings his songs about real experiences that seemingly happened yesterday," Nicks told *Variety* in late 2020. "He taps into real life. He doesn't make up stories. He tells the truth, and that is what I do." As a sign of her deep respect, she's often shown up during pivotal moments in his career to add musical support.

RIGHT & OVERLEAF
Harry Styles and inductee Stevie Nicks perform at the 2019 Rock & Roll Hall of Fame induction ceremony.

BLACK
LIVES
MATTER
END GUN VIOLENCE
END GUN VIOLENCE

A week after the release of his self-titled debut album, Styles played at the iconic Los Angeles club Troubadour. Nicks was on hand to make the concert extra special by collaborating with Styles on several songs, including his solo tune 'Two Ghosts', Fleetwood Mac's 1975 classic 'Landslide' and Nicks' 1981 solo song 'Leather and Lace'. Originally a duet with Eagles' Don Henley, the latter song showed off the chemistry between Nicks and Styles: the pair harmonized on the bittersweet song, their voices intertwining like they had been duet partners for decades.

It was far from the last time the pair would perform together. For starters, Styles sang 'The Chain' with Fleetwood Mac at a 2018 benefit show. Later, at Nicks' March 2019 Rock & Roll Hall of Fame induction as a solo artist – she had been inducted as a member of Fleetwood Mac in 1998 – Styles did the honours with a speech and performance. Sporting a bright blue Gucci velvet suit, he strapped on a guitar and duetted with Nicks on her 1981 hit 'Stop Draggin' My Heart Around', taking the vocal parts originated by the late Tom Petty. The gravity of this performance wasn't lost on him – Styles flashed the occasional smile at Nicks, but overall had a very serious look on his face as he harmonized carefully with her and belted out crucial lead vocal melodies.

His speech inducting Nicks was often hilarious. "Somewhere around 2005, 2006, this woman became God, I think we can all agree on that," he quipped. "On Halloween, one in seven people dress as Stevie Nicks. She is both an adjective and a verb. To quote my father, 'That was rather Stevie Nicks', and to quote my mother, 'I Stevie Nicks that shit so hard!'"

However, the speech was also earnest and heartfelt, reflecting the times they spent together and the wisdom she imparted. "If you're lucky enough to know her, she's always there for you," Styles said. "She knows what you need – advice, a little wisdom, a blouse, a shawl – she's got you covered. Her songs make you ache, feel on top of the world, make you want to dance, and usually all three at the same time. She's responsible for more running mascara

"If you're lucky enough to know [Stevie], she's always there for you," Styles said. "She knows what you need, advice, a little wisdom, a blouse, a shawl – she's got you covered."

– including my own – than all the bad dates in history combined."

Later in the year, Styles sang 'Landslide' again with Nicks at the Los Angeles Forum at the launch event for *Fine Line*. To say she liked this record was an understatement: in fact, before they went on stage, Nicks passed him a note that compared the the album to Rumours, Fleetwood Mac's legendary 1977 LP.. "We cried," she told *Variety*. "He sang those songs like he had sung them a thousand times. That's a great songwriter and a great performer."

Although the reception for Styles was, of course, delirious, the crowd response for Nicks when she strolled onstage was pandemonium. By now, old pros singing together, the version of 'Landslide' on this night was tender and moving; during the bridge the musicians even danced together and then clasped hands briefly. Styles, meanwhile, unleashed some different vocal harmonies – a sign of his growing confidence around Nicks and the strength of their friendship.

CHAPTER 6

HARRY'S HOUSE

novation

PAGE 110 Posing for photographers at the Venice Film Festival, 5 September 2022.

LEFT Live onstage at the iHeartRadio Secret Session, the Bowery Ballroom, New York City, 29 February 2020.

In 2020, Harry Styles was ready to launch a massive tour to promote his second album, *Fine Line*. Unfortunately, he was forced to scrap these plans after the emergence of the Covid-19 pandemic. Styles certainly wasn't the only musician in this situation. However, he felt the pause far more acutely than most, as it was the first time in roughly a decade he had *really* taken a break. The experience was disorienting, as he put it in one interview: "Suddenly, the screaming stopped."

This kind of go-go-go attitude had been ingrained in Styles because of his days in One Direction. As he told *Better Homes & Gardens*, being in the group was "all about how do you keep it going – and how do you get it to grow?" That mindset made him almost afraid to stop, he added. "There were so many years where, for me, especially in the band and the first few years coming out of it, I'd just been terrified of it ending," he said, "because I didn't necessarily know who I was if I didn't do music."

Given the fact that music venues were closed and in-person promotion was on pause, Styles had no choice but to figure out who he was outside of the spotlight. And so, while it was a leap of faith, he ended up chilling out from making music as the pandemic began. Styles moved into a house with three friends and did normal things like prep dinner and take walks. "Suddenly, you're forced to not be this musician guy," he told Zane Lowe. "You're forced to be a friend and a brother and a son. And I actually feel like I had a little bit of a chance to focus on that, at least for a moment."

Having this unscheduled stretch of time put Styles in a meditative mood, and he started to question his motivations for creation.

"[I] looked at what I turn to listen to and what I was watching and all that kind of stuff," he said, "and was like, 'What does it actually mean to make something? And what does it mean to me to make something as my job?'" This mindset lingered when Styles decided to start making music again. Alongside his long-time producers/co-writers, Kid Harpoon and Tyler Johnson, he moved into Rick Rubin's Shangri-La studio (where he recorded *Fine Line*), to see what kind of musical magic might emerge from being in such close quarters.

"We didn't really know what we were going in for," he told *Rolling Stone*. "It just felt like sitting at home doing nothing might feel better if we all moved in together and try to make some music." The first song he and Kid Harpoon wrote together for *Harry's House* – on the first day they were in the studio, no less – was 'Late Night Talking', a light-touch soul-funk number with smooth grooves and a sizzling chorus hook.

"In my house I'm playing fun music, sad music, I'm playing this, I'm playing that. It's a day in the life."

It was an encouraging sign – and a song that Styles saw as a guidepost of sorts for the rest of *Harry's House*. Once he started digging into the album, he had additional philosophical insights about the idea of home – and realized it was also less literal than he first thought. "[Home] wasn't about geographical location," Styles said. "It was much more of an internal thing ... [and] it felt like it took on this whole new meaning." More specifically, he pictured it more like a chronicle of his eclectic daily existence. "Imagine it's a day in my house; what do I go through?" he said. "A day in my mind; what do I go through? In my house I'm playing fun music, sad music, I'm playing this, I'm playing that. It's a day in the life."

To ensure the creative juices kept flowing, Styles and his band tried not to put too much pressure on themselves. Instead, they listened to their instincts and worked when they felt inspired. "We used to book a studio and be like, 'Okay, we've got it for two months, grind it out,'" Styles told Zane Lowe. "But some days you just don't want to be there, and eventually you've been in the studio so long, the only thing you can write about is nothing because you haven't done anything."

ABOVE Harry Styles, spotted in Venice, Italy, in 2022.

That meant Styles occasionally wrote songs both at home and in the studio (like 'Cinema') or recorded in fruitful bursts of inspiration. 'Daylight', for example, came together in a marathon all-night session that ended with Styles and his band at the beach watching the sunrise.

The sessions for *Harry's House* eventually went global. In addition to recording at Shangri-La, Styles and his band also hunkered down at Peter Gabriel's Real World Studios, just outside Bath, England. For good measure, he also drew inspiration from travels around Italy and France – countries he was able to visit once pandemic restrictions loosened – and time spent back at home in London.

The trip to Italy was especially profound. Styles spent a leisurely few weeks there by himself, decompressing and not worrying about keeping a schedule, before driving from Italy back to England by himself in a car owned by his late stepdad, Robin Twist, who had sadly passed away in 2017. On his trip, he listened to audiobooks, but also some of Robin's jazz CDs that were still in the car.

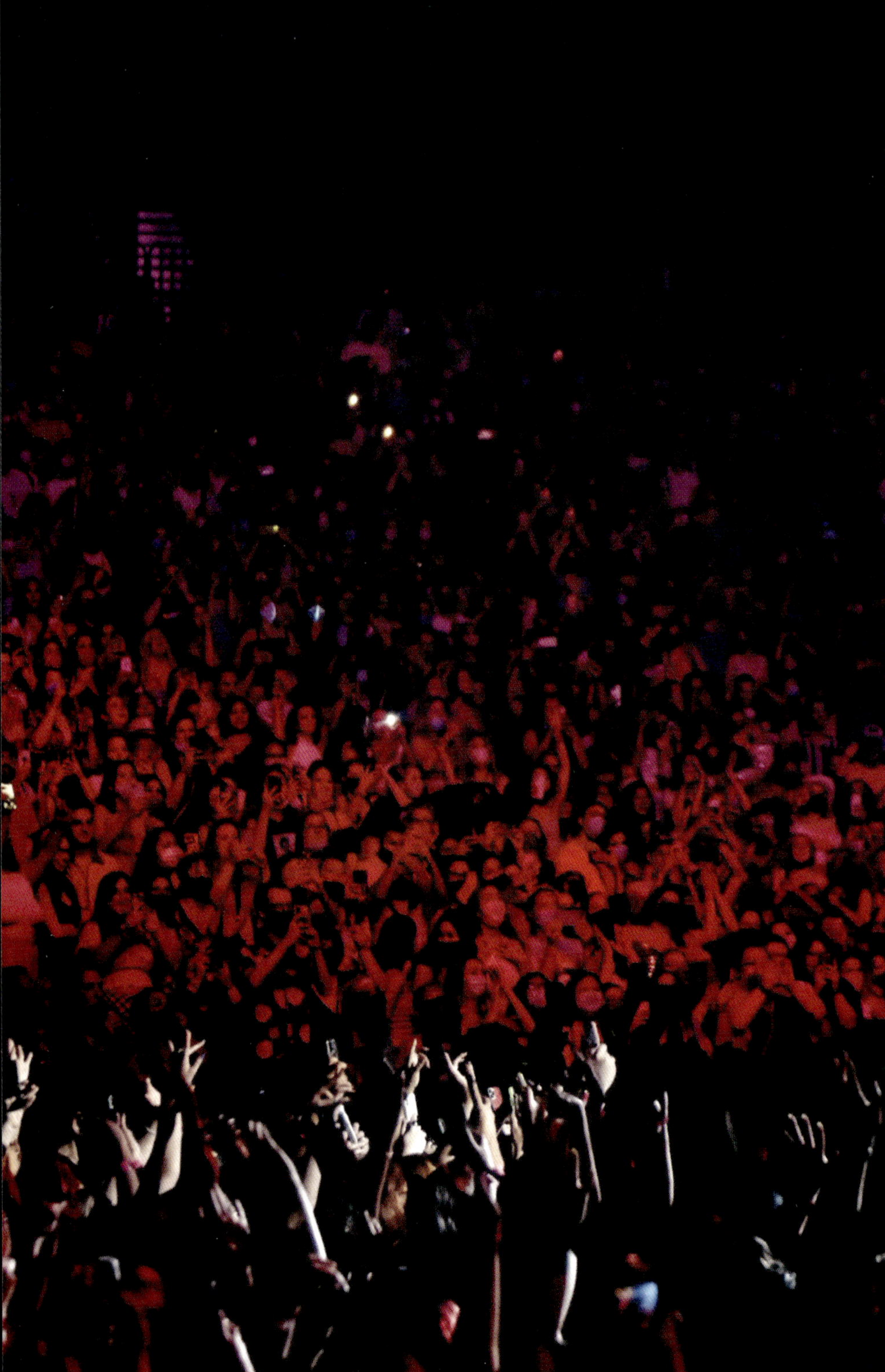

This experience was emotional, as it reminded him of the importance of family, and made him think about things like better work–life balance. "I felt like I did a family thing," Styles said. "And I think maybe for 12 years, family things have not always [been] the priority in maybe the way that they should've been, or I would like them to be more of going forward."

Fans didn't know it at the time, but *Harry's House* was done when Styles finally launched his Love On Tour concert tour in September 2021. In early 2022, he announced the album with a simple teaser video: sporting a flowing white shirt and blue jeans – the same outfit he sports on the album cover – and a slight smile on his face that exuded mystery, he walked out onto a small stage as an outline of a house was lifted around him. *Harry's House* received a thumbs up from none other than Styles' idol Joni Mitchell, who tweeted, "love the title" – coincidentally, she also has a song named 'Harry's House' – in addition to Daryl Hall and John Oates, who responded with a house emoji.

A week later, Styles released 'As It Was', the first single from *Harry's House*. Incredibly enough, it was the last tune he wrote for the album – composed in "my friend's front room in England's countryside," he told Hits Radio – and he initially wasn't sure if the song would make the final tracklist. In the end, however, it felt like a fitting song and sentiment to share. "It just felt like the thing I wanted to say, the thing I wanted to be doing and the kind of music I wanted to make coming back," he told radio platform Audacy.

'As It Was' starts with an adorable sample of Styles' five-year-old god-daughter, Ruby Winston, clamouring to tell the musician good night. Her voice is slightly pouty, a vibe explained by the fact that Styles apparently talked to her every night before she went to bed – but had skipped a call one night. ("She wanted to let me know that she was quite angry with me about it," he said in an interview.) From there, 'As It Was' blooms into a short-and-sweet song driven by pitter-pattering rhythms, pogo-ing grooves and a bouncing-ball synth hook. It's certainly reminiscent of past songs – most notably, clever Internet editors mashed up 'As It Was' with A-ha's new wave hit 'Take On Me' – but the music also boasted refreshing buoyancy.

Thematically, 'As It Was' also felt like something of a rebirth, albeit an ambiguous one. Speaking to NPR, Styles explained the song is "about metamorphosis and kind of losing yourself,

PREVIOUS PAGES & RIGHT Harry Styles onstage during the Love On Tour at the MGM Grand Garden Arena in Las Vegas, 4 September 2021.

LEFT Performing live onstage on day three of BBC Radio 1's Big Weekend, in Coventry, England, May 2022.

OVERLEAF Performing 'As It Was' at the 2023 Grammy Awards in Los Angeles.

"I feel like I'm putting music out from a real place of personal freedom."

finding yourself, embracing the fact that life hits you at different times, not when you expect it and, you know, change is scary." More specifically, the lyrics disclose that things in the world have changed – and although we're never explicitly told *why*, the narrator notes that the world is now simply "us". It's unclear whether that's a collective us or simply referring to people who have become a couple; Styles keeps things close to his chest, even though he notes directly in one lyric that he's *not* better off alone.

However, it's also unclear whether all of these changes are *good*, because 'As It Was' exudes more than a little hint of melancholy. But, in the end, the song feels like a perfect encapsulation of the evolution Styles went through with the pandemic – and the changes he was still trying to reconcile.

Appropriately, Styles told the SiriusXM *Morning Mash Up* he felt deep contentment upon the song's release. "I feel the most comfortable I've been with myself and happiest with what I'm making and the best I've felt about something that I'm making," he said, while adding, "I also feel really happy at the moment and I feel like it's the first time I feel like I'm making music and putting music out from a real place of personal freedom. And that is a really liberating place to [be] creating from and now putting it out."

Fans suspected there might have been another reason for this happiness, as they wondered whether several lyrics in the song (specifically ones mentioning two kids in context with a reference to not talk about the past) were veiled references to his then-girlfriend, the actress and director Olivia Wilde. The pair were

first spotted together holding hands at a January 2021 wedding. As the year unfolded, Wilde was spotted catching Styles' gigs (and sporting a Love On Tour concert T-shirt), and the couple were also photographed together on vacation.

The duo were still going strong upon the release of 'As It Was', despite heavy tabloid criticism about everything from their age difference (Wilde was a decade older than Styles) to her parenting skills; she shared two kids with her ex, the actor Jason Sudeikis. "When people see me not with my kids, it's always 'How dare she?'," Wilde told *Variety*. "I've never seen anyone say that about a guy. And if he is with his kid, he's a fucking hero."

Still, she and Styles decided to take the high road. "It's obviously really tempting to correct a false narrative," she told *Vogue*, in

ABOVE Jeffrey Azoff, Harry Styles, Kid Harpoon, Tyler Johnson and CEO of the Sony Music Group Rob Stringer pose with the Album of the Year award at the 2023 Grammy Awards ceremony.

reference to the scrutiny of their relationship. "I think what you realize is that when you're really happy, it doesn't matter what strangers think about you. All that matters to you is what's real, and what you love, and who you love." Months later, Styles noted he also preferred to keep his personal life, well, personal. "I've never talked about my life away from work publicly and found that it's benefited me positively," he told *Rolling Stone*. "There's always going to be a version of a narrative, and I think I just decided I wasn't going to spend the time trying to correct it or redirect it in some way."

That confidence transferred over to 'As It Was', which smashed streaming records and became Styles' second solo No. 1 hit in both the UK and the US, spending (respectively) 10 weeks and 15 weeks atop the singles charts. For good measure, it topped the Canadian singles charts for an impressive 18 weeks, and also reached No. 1 in Australia, Germany, Ireland, Switzerland and countless other countries.

Weeks later, on the day of *Harry's House* release, Styles performed a special concert at Long Island's UBS Arena. The streaming platform Apple TV broadcast the concert live, allowing fans to experience the show from anywhere. Styles ran through *Harry's House* and some other hits, to the great delight of fans. Prior to performing 'Grapejuice', he even addressed the crowd, noting, "Your job is to have as much fun as you possibly can. If you want to sing, if you want to dance. Please feel free to do whatever it is you want to do."

Harry's House earned 521,500 equivalent album units in the US during its first week on sale, the most successful week for any 2022 release until Taylor Swift's *Midnights* arrived months later. That same week, Styles also had four singles in the Top 10 of the *Billboard* Hot 100: the perennial hit 'As It Was', as well as 'Late Night Talking', 'Music For A Sushi Restaurant' and 'Matilda'. With this feat, he became the first British solo artist *ever* to achieve such a milestone. The only other British act overall to land this many songs in the US Top 10? The Beatles.

'Music For A Sushi Restaurant' also ended up having a memorable music video that resembled a mini-movie. In the science fiction-inspired clip, Styles portrays a half-human, half-squid creature who becomes the star attraction of a restaurant/club called Gill's Sushi. Despite his fabulous good looks and magnetic quality,

Styles is ultimately treated like, well, just another piece of fish. (Use your imagination as to what that might mean.) Much more lighthearted was the video for 'Late Night Talking', in which Styles' bed is a portal to other beds in all kinds of different places: a cheeky sleepover, an art gallery exhibit, a staid theatre and even a mobile bed that travels the streets of London.

RIGHT Harry Styles on the film set for *My Policeman*, in Brighton, England, 14 May 2021.

If all of this success wasn't impressive enough, Styles also co-starred in the 2022 film *My Policeman*, portraying a closeted policeman named Tom who strikes up a relationship with a man named Patrick (David Dawson) while marrying a woman (played by Emma Corrin). The film is set in 1950s England where, at the time, being gay was outlawed. "It's obviously pretty unfathomable now to think, 'Oh, you couldn't be gay. That was illegal,'" Styles told *Rolling Stone*. "I think everyone, including myself, has your own journey with figuring out sexuality and getting more comfortable with it."

Director Michael Grandage had previously told *Vanity Fair* he envisioned the film's sex scenes as "quite literally show[ing] something that was about 'lovemaking' in the broadest sense of the word," a sentiment Styles echoed to *Rolling Stone*. "There will be, I would imagine, some people who watch it who were very much alive during this time when it was illegal to be gay, and [Michael] wanted to show that it's tender and loving and sensitive." Styles' overall performance is indeed also very sensitive and generous, as he captures the conflicts within his character with nuance and grace.

Later in the year, he also co-starred in the dystopian drama-thriller *Don't Worry Darling*, which was directed and co-produced by Wilde. Set in the postcard-perfect California of the 1950s, the film finds Styles portraying a buttoned-up businessman named Jack who is married to Alice (Florence Pugh) – a whip-smart housewife who unravels a terrible secret, at great cost to everyone involved.

Styles and Wilde made news headlines again in November 2022 when it was announced the couple was "taking a break", as *People* reported. "He's still touring and is now going abroad. She is focusing on her kids and her work in LA," a source told the publication. "It's a very amicable decision." Still, he looked for the silver lining. In mid-December, Styles took to Instagram and posted a black-and-white photo of himself wearing a tracksuit and standing onstage before a show. "2022 changed my life," he wrote

as a caption. "I can't begin to thank all of you who supported me through it, I'll never forget it. I hope your end of year is filled with happiness and calm. Love you all."

Things would only get better in 2023, as Styles' hard work paid off when the 65th Annual Grammy Awards rolled around. 'As It Was' received four nominations – including in two of the biggest categories, Record of the Year and Song of the Year – while *Harry's House* was up for Album of the Year. At the February ceremony, Styles walked the red carpet in a rainbow-coloured patterned jumpsuit produced by EgonLab in collaboration with Swarovski. Incredibly, the suit featured 250,000 multicoloured crystals and took more than 150 hours to create.

Styles performed 'As It Was' with a stage design that featured a spinning platform similar to the one in the song's music video. Although Styles looked great – courtesy of a heavily fringed and sequinned silver Gucci suit – things didn't go entirely as planned on the performance side. As it turned out, the platform malfunctioned, in turn impacting the carefully planned choreography. Impressively, the performers improvised on the fly, on live television – and while certain moments did seem off, the overall performance came off fine.

Luckily, Styles had a much better night on the awards front. *Harry's House* won Grammy Awards for Best Pop Vocal Album and Best Engineered Album, Non-Classical. It also took home one of the major honours: Album of the Year, triumphing over full-length albums by ABBA, Adele, Bad Bunny and Beyoncé. Styles was the first British male solo artist to win this category since George Michael, who won the award for 1987's *Faith*.

Hecklers marred the sweet moment of Styles' big win somewhat by trying to interrupt him and protest his win because they thought other artists deserved the honour more. Some attendees in the audience came to his defence, however: Taylor Swift – who was also spotted grooving to the performance of 'As It Was' – and H.E.R. noticeably stood respectfully while Styles accepted his Grammy.

LEFT A film still from the movie *Don't Worry Darling*, 2022.

RIGHT: Harry attends the *Don't Worry Darling* red carpet at the Venice Film Festival, 2022.

If Styles was rattled, he didn't show it, as his acceptance speech was typically humble. "I've been so, so inspired by every artist in this category with me at a lot of different times in my life," he said. "I think on nights like tonight it's obviously so important for us to remember that there is no such thing as 'best' in music ... This doesn't happen to people like me very often and this is so, so nice."

In May 2023, Styles ended up releasing the fourth and final single from *Harry's House*, 'Satellite'. A sleek synth-pop song, it came with an adorable video written and directed by Aube Perrie, who also helmed the video for 'Music For A Sushi Restaurant'. This music video starred a little vacuum cleaner robot named Stomper who catches a glimpse of the Mars rover Curiosity, who has spent a decade exploring the Red Planet all by itself.

As Styles performs a show at the Los Angeles Forum, Stomper makes a break for it and has adventures all over the US. Ultimately, it ends up stargazing with a friend – Styles – outside a NASA building just as its batteries run out of juice. "Honored to be an inspiration to robots everywhere, @Harry_Styles," the official Twitter account for Curiosity tweeted after the video premiered.

Closing this chapter, he shared insights with Zane Lowe about 'As It Was' and its themes: "Everyone is changing, and I think there's no reason to not approach music that way, and kind of let it change and turn out differently than you started. You don't always get to realize something happens, and you kind of look at it and be, like, 'Wow', and then you get to decide whether that is devastating or brilliant, and accept the fact that it's probably both."

Treat People With Kindness

LEFT At the 2020 BRIT Awards, wearing a Treat People with Kindness badge.

When Harry Styles embarked on his first solo tour in 2017, he sold merchandise emblazoned with the phrase "Treat People With Kindness". The following year, he released a limited edition T-shirt with this phrase in rainbow-coloured text to celebrate Pride, with all proceeds going toward GLSEN, an American organization that strives to provide safe and inclusive schools for LGBTQ+ youth. In 2018, he also sold hair ties with the slogan during Live On Tour, where profits went to charity.

Incredibly enough, all of these things pre dated the song 'Treat People With Kindness', which ended up being on 2019's *Fine Line*. Co-written by Jeff Bhasker and Ilsey Juber, and featuring prominent lilting vocals from the duo Lucius and guitar from ex-Wings guitarist Laurence Juber, the upbeat song features a skipping-on-the-playground groove and delicate strings. Unsurprisingly, 'Treat People With Kindness' also boasts an underlying message that aligns with the title – that it feels good to be in a place where you're being kind, and being in this state of mind can even be a comfort during tough times.

Styles filmed one of his most memorable music videos for the song: shot in black and white as if to mimic an old-fashioned musical, it features him dressed in a dapper outfit while leading a big band. This eventually evolves into multiple highly stylized dance sequences, including memorable ones in tandem with the actress Phoebe Waller-Bridge. The video is an absolute delight, as it illuminates the joy in the song and demonstrates the power of dance to foster connection – an idea fans would later pick up on during Love On Tour performances of the song.

However, 'Treat People With Kindness' isn't just a song and a slogan. It's also an overarching ethos that informs his actions and fandom. Philanthropy is built into his concerts. By the end of Love On Tour, Styles had been able to donate more than £5 million (US$6.5 million) to charities around the globe, including Choose Love, Planned Parenthood, Physicians for Reproductive Health, Every Town for Gun Safety, Save the Children, International Rescue Committee and Black Minds Matter UK. He also partnered with the non-profit HeadCount to help 54,000 fans register to vote. This followed the impact of Styles' *first* round of tour dates, Live On Tour, which raised US$1.2 million for charity and also registered a significant number of new voters.

All of this builds on the causes Styles has supported over the years – a diverse list that includes being part of the #FirstSNOG campaign for the LGBTQ+ rights charity Stonewall, sponsoring water wells in India via Drop4Drop, and donating his hair to the Little Princess Trust, a charity that helps kids with hair loss obtain wigs. And this generosity is infectious: for example, fans celebrate Styles' birthday by coming together and raising money for charity. In 2019, that included more than US$30,000 for LGBTQ+ organizations like akt (originally the Albert Kennedy Trust), which helps LGBTQ+ 16–25 year-olds in the UK who are unhoused or dealing with an unhealthy or dangerous living environment.

At the end of the day, all of this kindness is wrapped up in gratitude, something Styles possesses in spades. "I hope you had as much fun as I did," Styles wrote on Instagram after the end of Love On Tour. "Look after each other, I'll see you again when the time is right. Treat People With Kindness. I love you more than you'll ever know."

RIGHT Performing at Rockefeller Plaza in New York, 2022.

CHAPTER 7

LOVE ON TOUR

PAGE 142 Performing One Direction's anthem, 'What Makes You Beautiful' with Lizzo as part of his headlining set at Coachella, 2022.

LEFT Onstage at the BRIT Awards in London, 2023.

It's said that good things come to those who wait. That's certainly the case with Harry Styles' second world tour, Love On Tour, which was supposed to start in 2020, but ended up being postponed and rearranged due to the Covid-19 pandemic and instead kicked off in September 2021. The delay ended up being for the best: Styles' popularity had skyrocketed in the meantime – among other things, he earned his first US No. 1 single with *Fine Line*'s 'Watermelon Sugar' – and he had had time to record an entirely new album, *Harry's House*.

Styles' concerts have long been known as welcoming safe spaces. As he himself told the audience at a November 2021 show in Detroit: "Please feel free to be whoever it is that you want to be in this room tonight." (He also expressed a similar sentiment at the rest of the tour dates.)

And Styles decided to help others express themselves outside of shows with the eco-conscious make-up and lifestyle brand Pleasing, which he launched in late 2021 with two partners: stylist Harry Lambert and his creative director Molly Hawkins. Pleasing's first offerings included four shades of nail polish, as well as primer serum and an eye and lip serum called the Pleasing Pen. "It's starting with nail polish, because that was kind of the birth of what it was for," Styles told *Dazed*. "Me seeing a colour on a flower or a wallpaper or something and thinking, 'Oh, I wanna put that on my nails.'" In subsequent years, the brand expanded into hand and nail cream, a skin spritz, apparel, genderless fragrances and lots more.

Love On Tour was also particularly special: coming after a very challenging few years for the world, the concerts became places that provided solace, community, much-needed connection and escapist fun. Styles responded to these vibes with energetic performances full of ecstatic, unselfconscious dance moves, charming stage banter and absolute gratitude for music.

The runaway popularity of Love On Tour allowed Styles to do some unique things, such as launch sold-out residencies in various cities – including an eye-popping 15 concerts at New York City's Madison Square Garden, 12 nights at the Los Angeles Forum and six-show residencies in both Chicago and Austin, Texas. When the tour finally wrapped in July 2023 in Italy, Styles had sold 5 million tickets for a total of US$617.3 million, making it easily one of the highest-grossing tours ever.

Unsurprisingly, although Love On Tour started out in support of *Fine Line*, it ended up also being a tour to promote *Harry's House*. Setlist-wise, this meant that the shows received a big overhaul after the release of *Harry's House*, with many of his early songs jettisoned in favour of newer works. (Never fear, however: Styles made sure One Direction's 'What Makes You Beautiful' *always* stayed in the setlist.)

Luckily, Styles' band could handle anything he threw at them. Although there were a few changes here and there as Love On Tour unfolded – among other things, Styles added a horn section, while keyboardist Niji Adeleye left after the 2021 dates and guitarist Madi Diaz hopped on for the 2023 UK and European legs – the core musical chemistry between the band members made all the difference.

Percussionist Pauli Lovejoy brought the rhythmic bustle and good vibes – he and Styles have been known to high-step in unison during 'Kiwi', for example – while bassist Elin Sandberg and keyboardists Yaffra and Ny Oh anchored the music with grooves and verve. Perhaps the most beloved member of the band, however, was

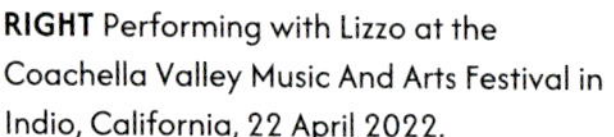

RIGHT Performing with Lizzo at the Coachella Valley Music And Arts Festival in Indio, California, 22 April 2022.

LEFT Performing live onstage with Shania Twain at Coachella 2022.

badass drummer/vocalist Sarah Jones, whose energy and personality made her a fan favourite. The only musician that equalled her popularity? Lead guitarist/vocalist Mitch Rowland, who happens to be married to Jones.

Styles' outfits also evolved over the course of the tour. He started off generally wearing tailored trousers and shirts in a rainbow of colours, but evolved his look to include things like feathered (or fringed) jackets, a series of jumpsuits in a heart pattern, or a vest-and-matching-trousers set with tassels or shiny decals. During 2022 Coachella Weekend 1 headlining gig, Styles sported a rainbow-sequin jumpsuit; he also brought out a very meaningful guest: country star Shania Twain.

As the opening chords of her late '90s hit 'Man! I Feel Like a Woman!' rang out, she appeared at the top of the stage and strutted down the stairs to trade off dance moves with Styles. In turn, he belted out lines from the song with gusto – a testament to his formative years listening to Twain. "In the car with my mother as a child, this lady taught me to sing," Styles said after the first song, then drew laughs with the next line: "She also told me that men are trash." However, he then became serious, telling Twain, "To you, to the memories you gave me with my mother, I will be forever grateful. I'm so grateful you're with us here tonight." The pair then did a tender version of Twain's 'You're Still The One'.

During his set at Coachella Weekend 2, Styles brought out Lizzo – whose song 'Juice' he had covered by himself *and* with Lizzo herself in early 2020 – for a cover of Gloria Gaynor's 'I Will Survive' and then One Direction's 'What Makes You Beautiful'. Wearing a gigantic fluffy pink coat and shiny magenta trousers, he held his own, especially on Gaynor's disco anthem, creating an empowering vibe.

Styles also debuted the *Harry's House* song 'Boyfriends' at Coachella. "It's both acknowledging my own behaviour [and] it's looking at behaviour that I've witnessed," Styles told Zane Lowe. "I grew up with a sister, so it's watching her date people and watching friends date people, and people don't treat each other very nicely sometimes."

Coachella wasn't the only memorable Love On Tour show. For example, Styles celebrated Halloween in 2021 at Madison Square Garden with a two-night event dubbed a Harryween Fancy Dress

Party. He lived up to the theme, dressing like Dorothy from *The Wizard of Oz* on night one – complete with ruby slippers, rosy cheeks and a humble blue-checked dress – and a Pierrot clown (think David Bowie's 'Ashes to Ashes' video) on night two. During the latter show, he also did a faithful, flirty cover of Britney Spears' 'Toxic' that brought the house down.

At the 2022 Harryween Fancy Dress Party in Los Angeles, he dressed like Danny Zuko from *Grease,* complete with a greaser hairdo and a black sleeveless shirt with the word "Harryween" in red glitter on the back. In honour of Olivia Newton-John, who played the role of Sandy in the film and had passed away in August 2022, he performed 'Hopelessly Devoted to You' from the movie. Weeks later, he did another meaningful tribute to a musician who had recently died – in Santiago, Chile, he covered Fleetwood Mac's 'Songbird' in honour of the lovely tune's writer, Christine McVie. Gorgeous and understated, the performance very much came from Styles' heart.

When Love On Tour reached Australia in March 2023, Styles nodded to his 2018 visit to the country and covered Rickie Lee Jones' 'The Horses' in Melbourne and Perth. And, during his second concert at Accor Stadium in Sydney, Styles had a special guest to give him a hand with the cover: Daryl Braithwaite, the Australian legend who had a massive hit in 1991 with his take on the song. After bowing down and doing an "I'm not worthy!" gesture toward Braithwaite, Styles and his band did an appropriately faithful cover of 'The Horses'; at one point, Braithwaite and Styles even harmonized in dreamy unity.

Beyond music, Love On Tour also featured some prominent show rituals. Dressing up was encouraged – and fans turned out with some amazing concert wear that mirrored Styles' bold fashion sense – and there was elevated banter. Among other things, Styles oversaw baby gender reveals and marriage proposals, and frequently joked with audience members. Song-wise, 'Treat People With Kindness' especially turned into a venue-wide dance party. Conga

Rituals at concerts are nothing new; in fact, they're a time-honoured tradition that bond people together into permanent friendships, creating what can often feel like a shared secret language. When you're going through rough times or seeking out your path in life, the bonding aspect of fandom provides comfort

RIGHT Taking to the stage dressed as Dorothy from *The Wizard of Oz*, complete with Toto the dog, as part of the Harryween Fancy Dress Party in 2021.

OVERLEAF A vision in vibrant pink, Harry Styles performs on the Coachella stage in 2022.

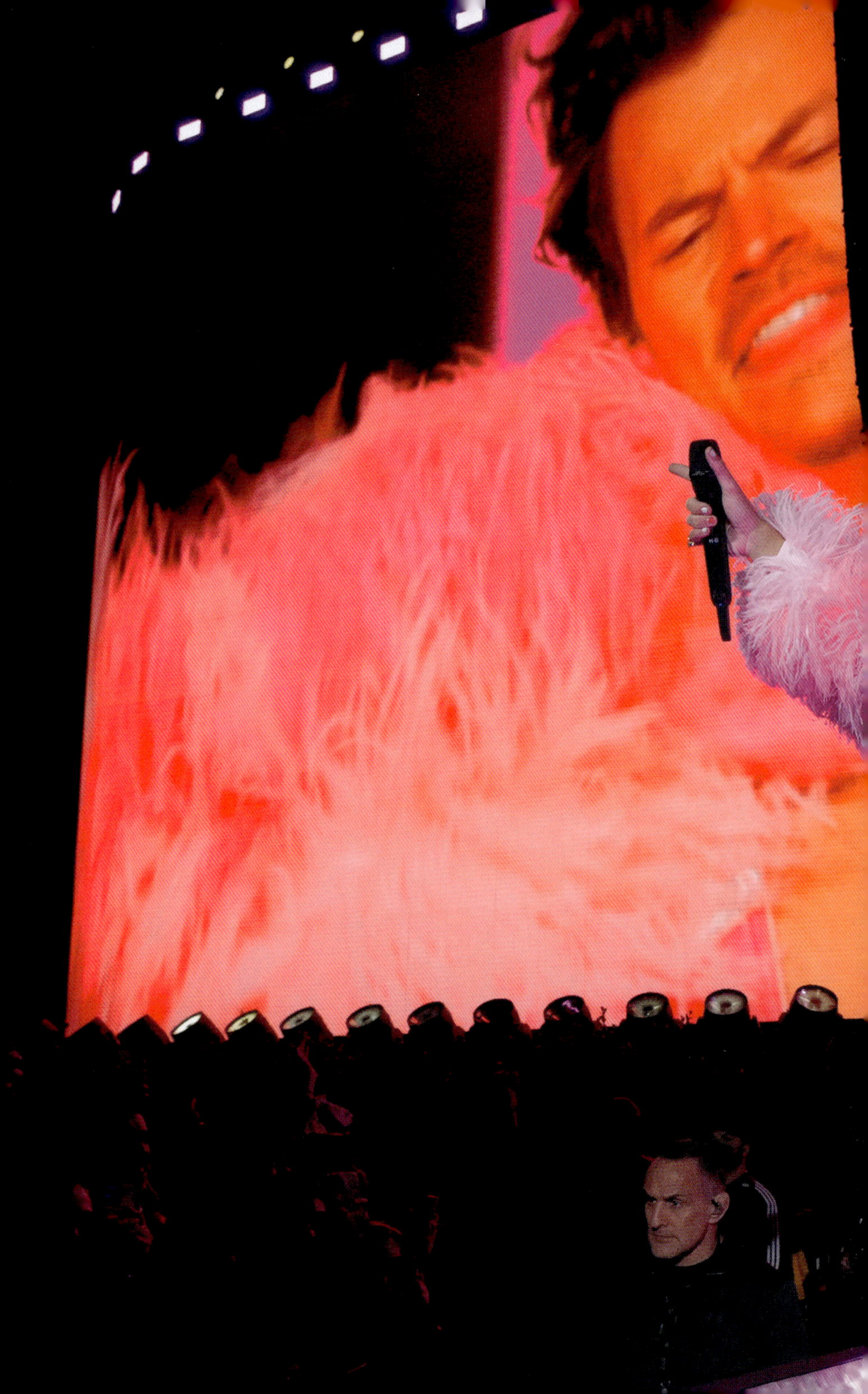

HOWARD
STERN

LEFT Harry visits SiriusXM's 'The Howard Stern Show' in New York City, 2022.

and meaning. Moreover, this welcoming environment especially spoke to why Styles' music and presence resonated so much. Love On Tour was an oasis of acceptance.

"It's definitely feeling like there's a space where people feel safe enough to have those big moments and obviously share them with a room full of people and share them with us, in a way," Styles said of his concerts during a 2022 interview with Howard Stern. "[That's] probably one of the things I'm most proud of."

Ever humble, Styles deflects taking credit for the "incredibly emotionally generous atmosphere" at his shows. "It's one of the first two things people comment on: 'I've just never been in an atmosphere like that'," he continued. "It feels so safe. It's like a family full of strangers who are feeling this free evening. It's kind of an escape. I think the fans create that atmosphere more so than me."

When Stern pushed back and said Styles was the "lightning rod" and "catalyst" for all of this, the musician responded, "I wouldn't say I was a catalyst. I'd say I'm more of a mirror. I only have that space onstage to feel free enough to be whoever I am because it's an environment that both the fans and people in my life, my friends, have created for me to feel like I can be whoever I want."

For years, Styles has worn or waved various flags given to him by fans during his shows – to name a few, the trans, pride, bisexual and lesbian flags. During Love On Tour concerts, he often used these flags to help fans come out. For example, if someone wanted to announce they were bisexual or a lesbian, he might very dramatically raise the corresponding flag above his head, amping up the drama with some tension-filled music, and then proclaim that the fan had officially come out. It often felt like he was knighting someone or otherwise bestowing a massive honour on them.

(To be fair, Styles helping fans come out is nothing new: at a 2018 show, he read a sign held up by a fan named Grace that read, "I'm going to come out to my parents because of you." Upon learning that her mother's name was Tina – and she was at a nearby hotel – he then decided to "tell Tina before you have the chance to". A few moments later, he bellowed a phrase that immediately became part of Styles fan lore: "Tina, she's gay.")

These moments aren't just deeply moving – they're a sign of Styles' allyship and the deep care and respect he has for fans, as well as his desire to make his concerts an inclusive environment. Coming out is often a process that's fraught with anxiety or uncertainty – but Styles eases these feelings by ensuring someone has an entire arena (or stadium) cheering them on in positive, affirming support.

When asked about the various flags, he told *Rolling Stone* in 2019, "I want to make people feel comfortable being whatever they want to be. Maybe at a show you can have a moment of knowing that you're not alone." Styles then acknowledged his privilege, adding, "I'm aware that as a white male, I don't go through the same things as a lot of the people that come to the shows. I can't claim that I know what it's like, because I don't. So I'm not trying to say, 'I understand what it's like.' I'm just trying to make people feel included and seen."

The latter desire also informed his public support for Black Lives Matter; for example, he affixed a sticker for the movement on his guitar and held up a Black Lives Matter flag during shows, including at an autumn 2021 concert in Los Angeles. These gestures were significant, as Styles wasn't always so vocal about his stance. In fact, he drew criticism from fans after ignoring a Black Lives Matter flag thrown onstage during a 2017 London show.

"I'm just trying to make people feel included and seen."

But after the May 2020 death of George Floyd – who was murdered by a white police officer in Minneapolis – Styles became more outspoken, writing on social media, "Being not racist is not enough, we must be anti racist. Social change is enacted when a society mobilizes. I stand in solidarity with all of those protesting." With no fanfare, he also showed up at a Black Lives Matter march in Los Angeles where he was pictured with friends.

"Talking about race can be really uncomfortable for everyone," Styles told *Variety* later in 2020. "I had a realization that my own comfort in the conversation has nothing to do with the problem – like that's not enough of a reason to not have a conversation." In other words, the introspection and self-reflection he experienced during the pandemic that influenced *Harry's House* also extended to his non-musical life.

"Looking back, I don't think I've been outspoken enough in the past," Styles continued. "Using that feeling has pushed me forward to being open and ready to learn. ... How can I ensure from my side that in 20 years the right things are still being done and the right people are getting the right opportunities? That it's not a passing thing?"

That thoughtfulness most of all permeated Love On Tour. And it was clear Styles didn't want the tour to end. On 22 July 2023, the tour wrapped up at the RCF Arena in Reggio Emilia, Italy. After the main set, Styles took to the piano and played a lengthy, untitled instrumental piece by himself that featured subtle horn and flute shading. It was sombre and reflective – and hinted at an intriguing new musical direction, if Styles wanted to go that route. But it was also achingly beautiful – the piece felt like he was giving Love On Tour a proper send-off.

After the tour, he released a video, *Love On Tour, Forever*, that included clips of fans from all over the world interspersed with behind-the-scenes footage and performance clips. The video was beautiful, as it showed off the community that sprang up around

BELOW A fan waiting to be admitted to the Love On Tour concert at Madison Square Garden, New York City, 2022.

Love On Tour – and demonstrated how diverse, beautiful and supportive Styles' fanbase is. "We want to help each other and just be kind to each other and love each other," a fan said in the clip. "Those friendships are gonna stay after the tour, and that doesn't end because the tour is ending. That's always going to be there." On Instagram, meanwhile, Styles shared additional thoughts about the tour. "It's been the greatest experience of my entire life. I feel so incredibly full and happy. It's all because of you. You have given me memories that will last a lifetime, more than I could have ever dreamed of. Thank you for your time, your energy, and your love."

After such a lengthy tour, it's understandable that Styles might not embark on another big trek again soon. But as the fan noted in the video, the impact of Love On Tour has endured even after the music stopped – and Styles for one couldn't be more thankful for the places his career has taken him. "Everything in my life has felt like a bonus since *X Factor,*" Styles told *Rolling Stone*. "Get on TV and sing. I never expected and never thought that would happen."

After Love On Tour ended in July 2023, Styles kept a low profile, save for the times when the tabloids spotted him hanging with rumoured then-girlfriend Taylor Russell or launching new Pleasing fragrances in London. In 2024, he continued to stay out of the public eye, until re-emerging onstage in June at Hyde Park, London as a special surprise guest with Stevie Nicks. The pair performed 'Landslide' and a cover of 'Stop Draggin' My Heart Around', wowing the crowd with moving performances.

LEFT Fans in front of the Ziggo Dome in Amsterdam, prior to the Harry Styles concert, July 2022.

OVERLEAF Performing at the BRIT Awards, O2 Arena, London, February 2023.

Later in the year, however, Styles experienced an unimaginable tragedy: the death of his One Direction bandmate Liam Payne. Styles posted a heartfelt statement of remembrance on social media, noting he was "truly devastated by Liam's passing ... The years we spent together will forever remain among the most cherished years of my life. I will miss him always, my lovely friend." The sombre note was a pointed reminder that Styles has never forgotten his roots, whether in music or in his upbringing – and navigates his life accordingly.

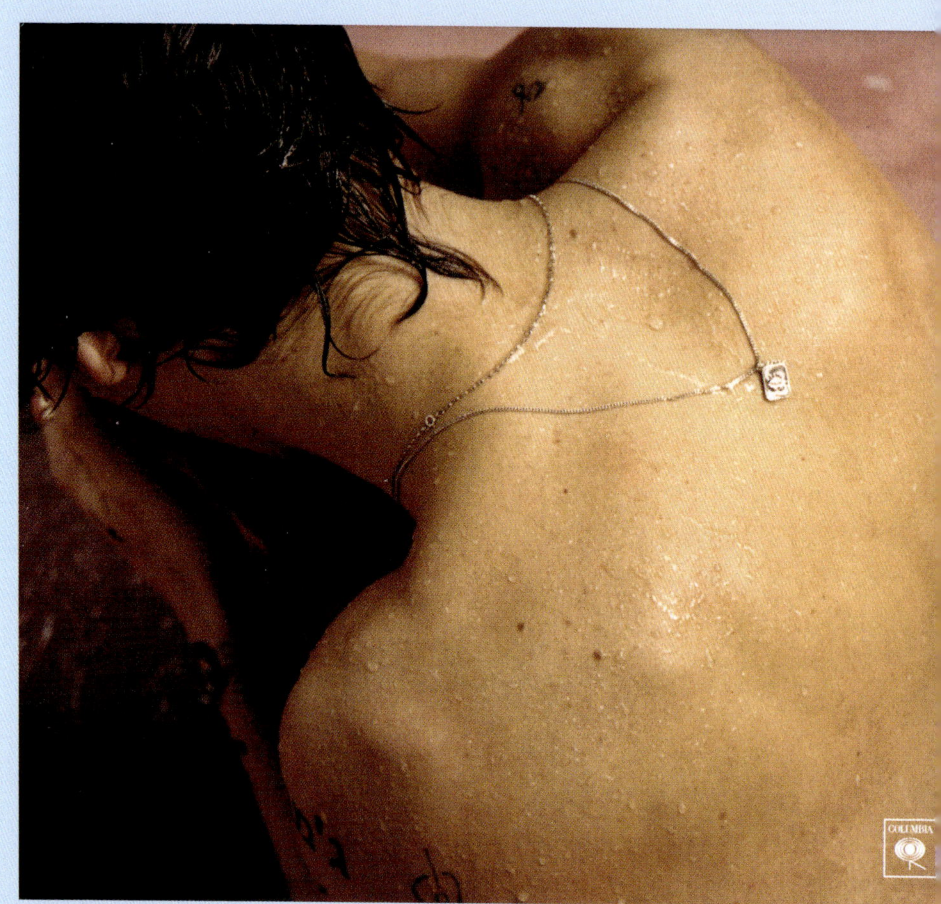
COLUMBIA

Harry Styles (2017)

Track List
'Meet Me in the Hallway'
'Sign of the Times'
'Carolina'
'Two Ghosts'
'Sweet Creature'
'Only Angel'
'Kiwi'
'Ever Since New York'
'Woman'
'From the Dining Table'

Released: 12 May 2017

A bold, confident solo collection indebted to warm 1970s pop-rock that established Styles as a contemporary pop icon.

Expectations were sky-high for Harry Styles when he announced his debut solo single, 'Sign of the Times', in March 2017 – and he delivered. A panoramic ballad blooming with languid beauty – think a gorgeous hot air balloon inflating to its full glory – the single combines solemn piano, scorched guitar twang, measured drums and a gospel choir. Styles alternates between an anguished falsetto and his usual keening midrange, shedding most vestiges of his glossy pop background.

Thematically, the song's lyrics suited the sonic grandeur. Styles told *Rolling Stone* that 'Sign of the Times' is quite a serious tune, "... written from a point of view as if a mother was giving birth to a child and there's a complication. The mother is told, 'The child is fine, but you're not going to make it.' The mother has five minutes to tell the child, 'Go forth and conquer.'" Fittingly, the song ends with a piano that sounds like an angel ascending to heaven. This was heady, serious stuff, and reviewers took notice, comparing 'Sign of the Times' to luminaries such as David Bowie, Pink Floyd and Elton John.

As it turns out, 'Sign of the Times' was something of an outlier on Harry Styles. Working mainly with a core group of songwriter-musicians, Styles crafted a taut collection of warm, classic-sounding pop-rock. 'Two Ghosts' resembles cozy singer-songwriter fare; 'Meet Me in the Hallway' is shimmering psychedelic pop; 'Sweet Creature' leans into golden-brown

RIGHT Harry performs in Sydney, Australia, 2017.

acoustic folk; and 'Only Angel' explodes like a swaggering Rolling Stones rocker.

Other additional instruments contribute pleasing variety: viola and violin snake through several tracks, while Styles himself contributes Omnichord in a few spots. In other words, Harry Styles contains the kind of earnest hits that populated the Top 40 in the 1970s – a bold update of One Direction's music, which itself took cues from various shades of 1970s rock.

Styles and his collaborators also very deliberately made sure the album wasn't too retro-sounding. This was important, as Styles was determined that the album reflected who he was – and what he had experienced in real life. "I didn't want to write 'stories'," he told *Rolling Stone*. "I wanted to write my stories, things that happened to me. The number-one thing was I wanted to be honest. I hadn't done that before."

In some cases, Styles was jaw-droppingly frank – for example, 'Kiwi' is about a vibrant, wild woman who's irresistible despite being rather over the top. Other songs address painful miscommunication or even break-ups. 'Meet Me in the Hallway' is about the agony of a crumbling relationship; 'Sweet Creature' addresses a tempestuous relationship; 'Two Ghosts', which Styles originally wrote for One Direction's last album, describes a couple who have lost their magic and now seem like invisible strangers to each other; and 'From the Dining Table' oozes with regret over a partnership that's fading away without closure.

In the end, *Harry Styles* was a blockbuster smash around the world, landing at No. 1 in the US, UK, Ireland, Mexico and countless other countries. Styles also made it abundantly clear that he was ready to make the transition from boy band member to solo artist – and had the confidence needed to forge an entirely new path for himself without missing a beat.

Fine Line (2019)

Track List
'Golden'
'Watermelon Sugar'
'Adore You'
'Lights Up'
'Cherry'
'Falling'
'To Be So Lonely'
'She'
'Sunflower, Vol. 6'
'Canyon Moon'
'Treat People With Kindness'
'Fine Line'

Released: 13 December 2019

Driven by self-aware lyrics and colourful nods to psychedelic rock, funk and R'n'B, *Fine Line* found Styles using bright strokes to redraw the boundaries of pop music.

Harry Styles was ready to be even bolder as he approached his second solo effort, *Fine Line*. Although the music is once again influenced by the 1970s – including flowery psychedelic pop, David Bowie's proto-glam, campfire folk and soulful funk – the album certainly doesn't play it safe. The sprawling 'She' is over six minutes long, with enigmatic lyrics, a zoned-out atmospheric vibe and some jagged-edge guitar work from Styles' musical collaborator Mitch Rowland. 'Sunflower Vol. 6' resembles a cross between quirky '80s new wave and Tame Impala-esque electronic pop.

And though Styles describes 'Canyon Moon' as "Crosby, Stills & Nash on steroids", the shimmying folk song was inspired even more by another denizen of the Laurel Canyon scene: Joni Mitchell. In fact, Styles was so committed to channelling her on the song that he took a dulcimer lesson from Joellen Lapidus, the same woman who built the dulcimer Mitchell used on 1971's *Blue*.

Lyrically, *Fine Line* found Styles taking a cue from Mitchell and reflecting candidly on his life in the previous few years. While he gave *Rolling Stone* a pithy answer about the album's meaning ("It's all about having sex and feeling sad"), it's fair to say he experienced quite serious ups *and* downs while

COLUMBIA

Spotify

“It’s all about having sex and feeling sad.”

making it – and extreme ones at that. “What I hadn’t really experienced before during the making of this record, the times when I felt good and happy were the happiest I’ve ever felt in my life,” he revealed to Zane Lowe. “And the times when I felt sad were the lowest that I’ve ever felt in my life.”

‘Golden’ and ‘Adore You’ talk about a relationship in happier times, while the title track addresses trying to find equilibrium within a tumultuous dalliance. Other songs are more explicitly about a broken relationship. His break-up with the model Camille Rowe informs ‘Cherry’, a wounded and jealous song written from the perspective of someone who isn’t thrilled their ex has moved on and is thriving; the lyrics even explicitly ask them not to call their new partner “baby”, a meaningful nickname.

However, Styles was just as honest about his own faults, particularly on ‘To Be So Lonely’, which also touches on his relationship with Rowe. In a callback to ‘Cherry’, he says he doesn’t deserve to be called “baby” any more – besides, it’s too painful anyway – and admits he was stubborn and jealous. Styles also notes he’s also reached the acceptance stage of the break-up; after getting all of the self-flagellation and sulking out of his system, he’s okay with the chapter closing on the relationship.
It’s no coincidence that maturity and depth are also two hallmarks of *Fine Line*. Styles had found the right balance of like-minded creative souls and collaborators, and was more confident about his songwriting instincts, giving him the space he needed to flourish. As a result, *Fine Line* amplified both his innate pop sensibilities and spirit of adventure – and became another enormous hit, reaching No. 1 in the US, Australia, New Zealand and multiple other countries, and peaking at No. 2 in the UK.

LEFT Harry attends the Spotify private listening event, celebrating the release of his album *Fine Line*, in Los Angeles, 2019.

COLUMBIA

Harry's House (2022)

Track List
'Music For a Sushi Restaurant'
'Late Night Talking'
'Grapejuice'
'As It Was'
'Daylight'
'Little Freak'
'Matilda'
'Cinema'
'Daydreaming'
'Keep Driving'
'Satellite'
'Boyfriends'
'Love Of My Life'

Released: 20 May 2022

An introspective, dynamic album that reflects Styles' love of sleek R'n'B/funk and airy pop – and his willingness to be a vulnerable songwriter.

Harry's House is breezy and meditative – the sound of catharsis and introspection colliding in what some consider Styles' best solo album yet. Among other things, the album reflects Styles' weekly commitment to therapy, which led him to insights about himself. In 'Little Freak', he looked back at past failed relationships, while in tunes such as 'Cinema' and 'Grapejuice' he muses about the nuances of new love. These moments are often delightfully detailed. 'Keep Driving', for example, chronicles the intimate details of a relationship with playful language about a cosy breakfast: pancakes with syrup, coffee, hash browns and eggs. 'Love Of My Life' is about his love for England, even though it also scans like it's about a relationship.

Title-wise, *Harry's House* is a nod to *Hosono House*, the 1973 solo LP by the influential Japanese musician Haruomi Hosono. Although known for his work with the electronic music pioneers Yellow Magic Orchestra, Hosono also played in several bands – including the psychedelic-leaning group Apryl Fool and folk rockers Happy End – and is associated with the Japanese genre city pop; the latter takes influence from (among other things) late-'70s/early-'80s rock, funk, soft rock, and R'n'B.

The sound of *Harry's House* especially takes influence from the latter genre, as multiple songs boast humid funk-R'n'B grooves: the mid-1980s homage 'Cinema', soft-glow soul-pop gem 'Daydreaming' and the horn-peppered 'Music For A Sushi

Restaurant'. Other moments hew toward dreamier fare ('Little Freak'), while 'Love Of My Life' and 'Matilda' are deliberately stripped back; the latter takes cues from indie-folk – and features cello from indie star Dev Hynes – while the former feels like a classic torch song. For good measure, John Mayer plays guitar on two songs, while Ben Harper contributes guitar to 'Boyfriends'.

Prior to making *Harry's House*, Styles also started listening to classical and instrumental music, including works by the jazz pianist/composer Bill Evans and composer Samuel Barber as well as the music of *Swan Lake*. Accordingly, *Harry's House* uses its instrumental palette for emotional impact, in large part by employing deliberate dynamics.

This thoughtful approach paid dividends. *Harry's House* ended up winning a slew of awards, including Album of the Year at the MTV Video Music Awards and British Album of the Year at the Brit Awards, along with three Grammy Awards. In a roundabout way, it seems like Styles found his happy place by taking a break from the public eye.

RIGHT Harry Styles onstage during the 65th Grammy Awards at the Crypto.com Arena on 5 February 2023 in Los Angeles.

DALEY

PICTURE CREDITS

Getty Brian Rasic, Shirlaine Forrest/WireImage, Dave J Hogan, Kevin Mazur/WireImage, Jason Merritt, iHeartMedia, Zak Kaczmarek, ARIA, Frazer Harrison, Victoria's Secret, Dave J Hogan, Kevin Mazur, SiriusXM, Karwai Tang/WireImage, John Shearer, Sandbox Entertainment, Kevin Winter, The Recording Academy, Anthony Pham via, MEGA/GC Images, Vittorio Zunino Celotto, Gareth Cattermole, Theo Wargo, HS, Gilbert Carrasquillo/GC Images, Cindy Ord, SiriusXM, Alexi Rosenfeld, Karwai Tang/WireImage, Scott Barbour, ARIA, Rich Fury, Spotify, Mike Coppola/WireImage, Saira MacLeod/WWD via, Anthony Pham via,Dave J Hogan, Kevin Mazur, ABA, Steve Jennings, Sony Music, Kevin Mazur, The Recording Academy, Jeff Spicer, Dave Hogan, Al Pereira/WireImage, Jason Merritt, iHeartMedia, Al Pereira/WireImage, Terence Patrick/CBS via, James Devaney/GC Images, Kevin Mazur, HS, GORC/GC Images, Kevin Mazur, Casamigos, Kevin Mazur, HS, Matt Winkelmeyer, Robyn BECK / AFP, ROBYN BECK/AFP via, Kurt Krieger/Corbis via, Kevin Mazur/MG19, The Met Museum/Vogue, Dominique Charriau/WireImage, Rich Fury, Spotify, Kevin Winter, The Recording Academy, Fin Costello/Redferns, Theo Wargo, The Rock and Roll Hall of Fame, Joseph Okpako/WireImage, Kevin Mazur, SiriusXM, Jun Sato/WireImage, Anthony Pham/via, Joseph Okpako/WireImage, Neil Mockford/GC Images, Karwai Tang/WireImage, CBS via, Alexi Rosenfeld, Cindy Ord, SiriusXM, Theo Wargo, HS, Michael Buckner/Variety via, Leon Bennett, Neil Mockford/GC Images Alamy PA Images / Alamy ZUMA Press, Inc. / Alamy Associated Press / Alamy PA Images / Alamy Evan Agostini/Invision/AP ARCHIVIO GBB / Alamy Stock Photo WENN Rights Ltd / Alamy Stock Photo, Vinyls brinkstock / Alamy Stock Photo, Doug Peters / Alamy Stock Photo, MediaPunch Inc / Alamy, Matt Crossick / Alamy Stock Photo, bEvan Agostini/Invision/AP, Byron Purvis/AdMedia/Sipa USA, © Jason Moore/ZUMA Wire/Alamy Live News, © Twentieth Century Fox Film Corp. All rights reserved. /Courtesy Everett Collection, AP Photo/Mark Humphrey, Charles Sykes/Invision/AP, Amy Harris/Invision/AP, Scott Garfitt/EMPICS/Alamy Live News, PJR news, Scott Garfitt / Alamy Stock Photo, Vianney Le Caer/Invision/AP, AP Photo/Chris Pizzello, Moviestore Collection Ltd / Alamy Stock Photo, JGY/Alamy Live News Shutterstock Mcpix Ltd, Richard Young, Ken McKay, Mcpix Ltd, Ken McKay, Ken McKay/Talkback Thames, Startraks, David Fisher, Broadimage, JM Enternational, Mirco Toniolo - Errebi, David Fisher.

LEFT Harry wears a broadcloth chore jacket set with a strawberry pin and a Cochrane white vest by S.S. Daley at the label's Spring/Summer 2025 fashion show in September 2024.

OVERLEAF Harry's Wall at the Twemlow viaduct in Holmes Chapel, Cheshire. There is now a dedicated fan wall to avoid damage to the Grade II-listed landmark.

YOU BRING ME HOME
TPWK
LUCE
ELLIE JANA TPWK LIBBY LIV MEG 2020
ARGENTINA
HANNAH
HARRY
CHARLIE
KATIE
WE'RE ALL
A LITTLE BIT
GAY
AREN'T
WE!
FRASIE
WE LOVE YOU
BRAZIL
GRACE G
MAMÁ
TPWK